KNITS

FROM AROUND NORWAY

NINA GRANLUND SÆTHER

KNITS

FROM AROUND NORWAY

OVER 40 TRADITIONAL KNITTING PATTERNS
INSPIRED BY NORWEGIAN FOLK-ART COLLECTIONS

TRAFALGAR SQUARE
North Pomfret, Vermont

First published in the United States of America
in 2021 by
Trafalgar Square Books
North Pomfret, Vermont 05053

Originally published in Norwegian as *Strikk fra Hele Norge*.

The instructions and material lists in this book were carefully
reviewed by the author and editor; however, accuracy cannot be
guaranteed. The author and publisher cannot be held liable for
errors.

ISBN: 978-1-64601-047-9
Library of Congress Control Number: 2021933233

Interior Design and Layout: Sissel Holt Boniface
Cover Photo: Eivind Rohne
Cover Design: RM Didier
Translation into English: Carol Huebscher Rhoades

Printed in China
10 9 8 7 6 5 4 3 2 1

TABLE OF CONTENTS

Something Old, Something New

It can be difficult to trace our path as knitters back through history. In the past, textiles of all kinds were often used until they were completely worn out, or turned in for a low price—factories needed fibers that could be re-carded and reused. Everyday textiles very seldom ended up in museums. The items that have been preserved were, for the most part, worn for parties and special occasions.

Fortunately, there are also paintings and photographs documenting clothing trends in earlier times. Some were inspired by colors in a flower bouquet, others by something cool in a fashion magazine. I'm always fascinated by older textiles—clothing and other fabric items that were at one time elegant and rich in color tend to fade and felt, and there's something special about the patina of faded colors. Perhaps it's because I know how much time and effort is behind each individual garment.

In this book, I've once again been on the hunt for knitted garments, or the traces of them, around Norway. Not to copy them stitch for stitch, but to find inspiration. A small pattern element can be enlarged and knitted with heavier yarn and larger needles. Or it can be placed in a new context. There are innumerable examples to work with, full of gorgeous, timeless pattern elements—and I've catalogued those examples here. This book isn't just about my designs, it's about history.

At a time when you can buy almost anything, and textiles, for the most part, are made at low costs in countries far away, I hope you all experience the joy of creating something with your own hands, a joy that lies in the design and construction of a garment. Yes, it takes time, and it can be really difficult ... but when it's done, you'll be rewarded with something unique, something irreplaceable. Something that will last; something worth all your time and effort. Something that carries on cultural traditions, and brings the things that matter the most to life.

Nina Granlund Sæther

Nina Granlund Sæther on the internet: www.hjertebank.no
Facebook: Hjertebank Nina Granlund Sæther. Instagram: @ninagranlundsather

TIPS BEFORE YOU BEGIN

Charts: All charts in this book are read from right to left and from the bottom up.

Garment Care: To give your garment a professional look, you should lightly steam press it, or wash it in lukewarm water with wool-safe soap and block it. You can buy sock blockers, or you can dry socks flat. Shawls or lace edges can be pin-blocked or stretched out with blocking wires. Leave items pinned out until completely dry.

Decreasing on the right side (= left-leaning decrease): Slip 1, knit 1, pass slipped stitch over (sl 1, k1, psso) or ssk (see Abbreviations).

Decreasing on the left side (= right-leaning decrease): Knit 2 together (k2tog).

Weaving in ends: It's important to weave in ends well. You can do that by sewing ends through the stitch loops on the wrong side. Begin going one way; turn and sew back. Make sure the end doesn't show on the right side.

Reinforced yarns for socks: There are various yarns specifically spun for socks and stockings. Generally, these contain polyamide (nylon) or polyester to make the yarn more durable. Often, these yarns are also superwash so the wool won't felt.

Norwegian Spelsau yarns were previously the sock yarns of choice. Spelsau fleece has both a soft undercoat and a long, strong outercoat, which makes for an especially strong yarn. Many small mills in Norway spin and sell this type of yarn.

Both horse and goat hair have been used to reinforce sock heels and soles on "ragg socks" (the Norwegian word ragg refers to tangled goat hair). Women's hair was also used. These days, though, it's more common to use nylon-reinforced yarn for socks. However, you might not want to knit with a blended-fiber yarn. In that case, you can carry along another strong yarn or thread, for the whole sock or on the heels and toes, whichever you prefer. Finely-spun Spelsau—for example, Røros embroidery thread—is good for that purpose, but the resulting knitted fabric will be considerably stiffer. You could also use silk sewing thread or nylon buttonhole thread, available in various colors in sewing supply shops. Sewing thread is less bulky than embroidery thread, and will be less visible.

Yarn: The yarns listed in the patterns are recommendations. If you use another yarn, make sure you match the listed gauge so the result will be the right size.

Necklines: Making a neat neckline on a knitted garment can be a bit of a challenge. Here's a method you can use: Find a garment with a neckline you like. Fold a piece of paper in half and lay it on the garment. Trace the neckline—first the front, and then the back.

Make sure the tracing is symmetrical and centered. Fold the paper in half again and cut away any unevenness. Mark the center front and center back as well as the shoulder seams. Don't forget that this pattern template can be used more than once, if you like the results. There's also a sample template on page 10 you can try, if you want to.

When you have lightly pressed the garment-in-progress, you should find the center front and mark it with basting thread. Lay your template on top and baste around it in a contrast-color thread. After finishing the front, do the same on the back.

Remove the paper template and machine-stitch above the basting thread, or completely inside it if you prefer. I recommend fine zigzag lines; it's also a good idea to sew two lines on each side to ensure the stitches won't slide out. You can also use vlieseline on the back. Hand-sewing or crochet will also work.

If your garment has set-in sleeves, you should also sew around the armholes. Join the shoulders by stitching or knitting them together, if you haven't already.

The next step is to pick up and knit stitches for the ribbing. Pick up and knit stitches about ¼ in / .5 cm outside the basting line. Use a crochet hook to bring each stitch through and onto the knitting needle. At the center front, it'll be easy to see where to pick up stitches, but it's trickier at the sides. Usually, you'll pick up 3 stitches for every 4 rows in length. Work carefully.

After you've picked up stitches all around the neckline, make sure everything looks right. Trim away excess fabric following the basting and work the neckband as instructed. If you're making a doubled band, you can use it to hide the seam and cut edges. After completing a doubled neckband, sew it down on the wrong side with loose stitches so it isn't too tight when you pull the sweater over your head.

1 Pin the template to the sweater. Make sure the center front of the template aligns with the center front of the sweater. Also make sure the shoulder seams lie correctly. Use a contrast-color thread to baste all around.

2 Once you've sewn all around the template, you can remove it.

3 Double-check to make sure the neckline is centered on front and back.

4 Crochet around so the stitches don't slide out. Hand- or machine-stitch inside the basting thread.

5 Use a crochet hook to pick up stitches around the neckline. Make sure everything looks right.

6 Trim away any excess fabric.

7 Work the neckband as instructed in the pattern.

8 Fold the band over the cut edge and sew it down on the wrong side.

9 Gently steam press the garment under a damp pressing cloth.

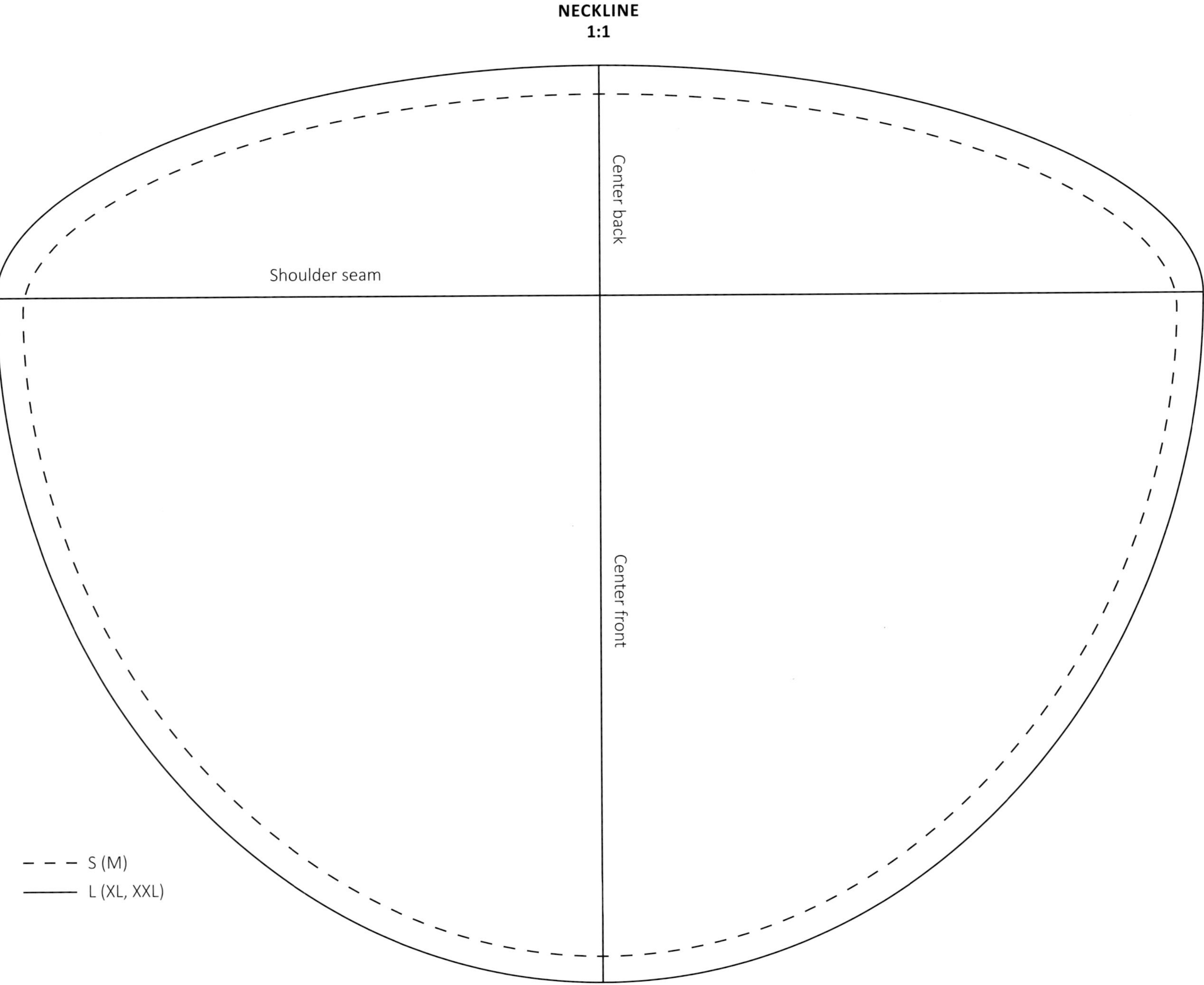

NECKLINE
1:1
Center back
Shoulder seam
Center front
S (M)
L (XL, XXL)

Heels: All feet are different. Some people have narrow feet; others have wide ones. The height to the ankle also varies. There are many ways to knit heels, and the heel type I recommend depends on how each "sits" on the foot. Knitting a heel isn't difficult once you have the hang of it, but it might be a little challenging the first time. Find someone who can help you, or check the internet—there are a lot of helpful tutorial videos out there.

If you're going to knit a heel and you don't have a lot of experience, I recommend placing the instep stitches on an extra circular needle or strand of scrap yarn. The stitches on each end could get stretched out if they remain on your working needles. If you're using scrap yarn, it'll be easier to avoid holes and loose stitches at the sides.

Heel flap: You have several options for picking up stitches along the sides of a heel flap. You can, for example, lift one side of the chain stitch directly onto the knitting needle—that's the easiest way. You can pick up either one or both of the chain stitch loops. Do as you please. Picking up both loops works quite well; that's the method I personally prefer. You can also pick up the stitches in a twisted orientation, or knit them through the back loops to twist them on the next round.

Chain stitches: When you knit a heel flap, you can make chain stitches along each side. Begin each row with 1 stitch slipped as if to knit. This method is worked back and forth.

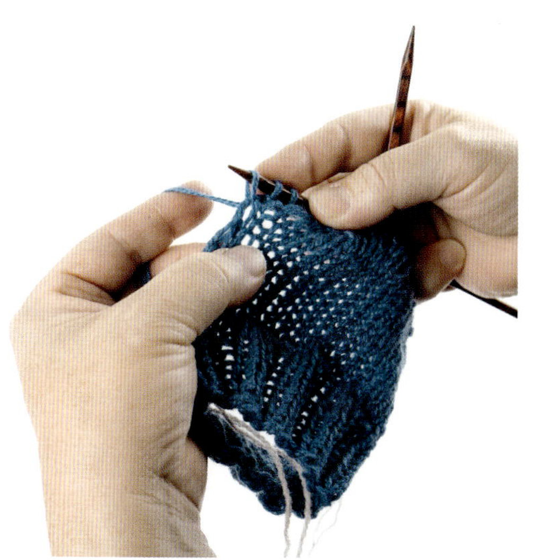

Pattern knitting: When working patterns with two or more colors, it's important not to let the colors change places in your hands. If the strands change position relative to each other, you'll soon be able to see that the knitting doesn't look the same anymore.

Casting on: There are many ways to cast on. Choose a method you like. The cast-on should be firm but not tight.

Needles: The items in this book are worked on circular needles, either in the round or back and forth, or else on five double-pointed needles. If you prefer, you can use the magic loop method with a long circular instead of double-pointed needles.

Three-needle bind-off for knitted joins: Joining the shoulders on a cardigan or pullover isn't always easy. Stitches you've bound off first can be sewn together, but that leaves a slightly

lumpy seam. You can sew the stitches without first binding off by using Kitchener stitch, but you have to be careful to keep the stitches in the right order. An even easier method that produces a smooth seam is to knit the pieces together.

When you've finished knitting the garment, find the sides and turn the garment inside out so the right sides of front and back face each other. The needles should be held parallel. You'll need a third needle in the same size. Knit two together, joining the first stitch of each needle. *Knit the next two stitches together. Bind off as usual by passing the first joined stitch on the right needle over the second.* Repeat from * to * until you've joined and bound off all the stitches.

In most cases, the length of the foot can be adjusted. If the socks are slightly too large and were worked in untreated wool (that is, not superwash), you can felt them. In the past, it was common to felt socks to make them warmer and more durable.

Shoe Sizes

U. S. / Euro	Foot Length	Approx Age
1½-5½ / 17-21	4-4¾ in / 10-12 cm	1-2 years
6-9½ / 22-26	5¼-6¼ in / 13-16 cm	2-4 years
10½-13½ / 27-31	6¾-7½ in / 17-19 cm	5-6 years
1-4 / 32-36	8-8¾ in / 20-22 cm	7-10 years
6½-9½ / 37-40	9-9¾ in / 23-25 cm	Women's
8-11 / 41-44	10¼-11 in / 26-28 cm	Men's
12-14 / 45-48	11½-12¼ in / 29-31 cm	Men's XL

Check your work on the right side to make sure the patterns align. If the garment had a steek, bind off those stitches. Join the other shoulder the same way. If you knitted a pullover, you can join all the way across.

The same technique can be used on the underarms. Whether you've worked a round or raglan yoke, you'll usually have 10 stitches set aside for each underarm on the body and sleeves. Instead of joining them with Kitchener stitch, you can hold the pieces with right side facing right side and knit them together with three-needle bind-off.

I-cord: Cast on 3 or 4 stitches. *Bring the yarn to needle tip and knit. *At the same time*, tug the yarn on the wrong side. Repeat from * until the cord is desired length.

Socks: The patterns have three sections: leg, heel, and foot. The leg usually begins with a ribbed cuff or edging and the foot ends with toe shaping.

Begin and end each round at the center back on the leg or centered on the sole.

The first needle holds the stitches of the left half of the back; the second needle, the left half of the front; the third needle, the right half of the front, and the fourth needle holds the right half of the back.

Sock sizes: If a sock pattern in this book lists only one sock size, that size will typically match a women's shoe size U. S. 6½-9 / Euro 37-40. If you want a smaller sock, you can choose a finer yarn and smaller needles. Conversely, if you want bigger socks, choose a heavier yarn and larger needles.

Bands on pullovers and cardigans: There are several ways to make bands; I recommend knitting or crocheting them before a steek is cut open up the front. That lessens the chance of stitches sliding out, and makes it easier to ensure that the left and right bands match. The cut steek edges can be covered with a knitted or crocheted facing or a ribbon.

Gauge: If you want your finished garment to be the right size, it's important to maintain the correct gauge. If you knit too loosely, the garment will be too big. In that case, try smaller needles. On the other hand, if you knit too tightly, you should try larger needles.

Sizes: Most cardigans and pullovers in this book can be worked in sizes S, M, L, XL, and XXL. Socks and mittens will usually be offered in two sizes. The chart may be the same for more than one size, in which case the sizing is adjusted by a change of gauge.

Seaming facings/edgings: Wash the fabric before you begin sewing it on. Begin with side pieces, marked 1 and 2. Trim a strip about 1½-2 in/ 4-5 cm wide with ⅜ in / 1 cm seam allowance on each side. Pin the fabric to the knitted garment and sew down on the long side furthest from the neckline, using small over-hand stitches. Next, shape to the neckline and trim away any excess fabric before you fold the facing in and pin it to the edge.

Do the same on the back, marked 3. The fabric strip should be 2¾ in / 7 cm wide with ⅜ in / 1 cm seam allowance on each side. Begin on the long side furthest from the neckline. Make sure the strip is long enough at the sides to cover the facing you have sewn on. Fold it in and pin. Sew the long side first. Fold in the corners and sew down firmly to the facing at the sides. Shape to the neckline and trim away any excess fabric before you fold the facing in and pin it in place.

Trim a strip about 2-2½ in/ 5-6 cm wide with ⅜ in / 1 cm seam allowance on each side for the bands. Pin it in place and sew down the edge, beginning at the neckline.

Lay a ribbon along the edge, all the way around; pin it down and sew it to the facing. Some prefer to place it edge to edge, while others prefer to fold the ribbon around the edge. Make sure there's enough ribbon to allow you to ease it in at each corner.

It's best to attach buttons through both the knitted fabric and the facing, and to thread the buttons through a twill tape or something similar. Sew down the ribbon to the facing.

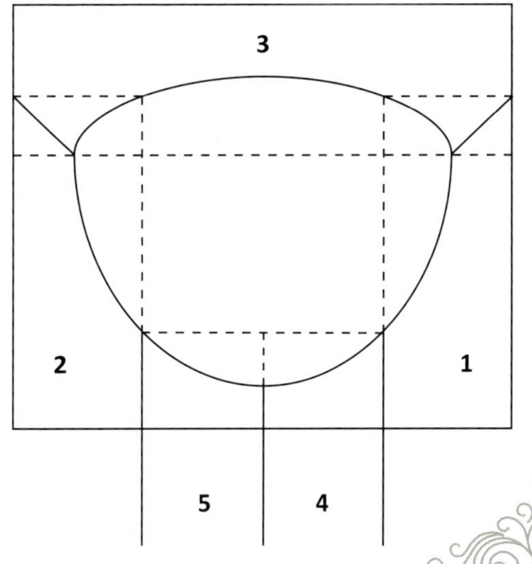

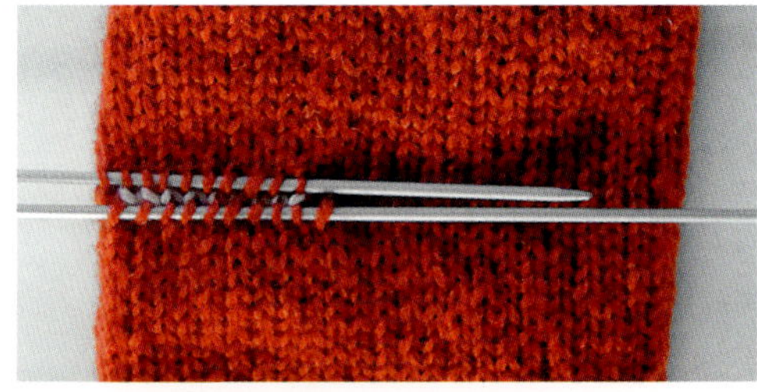

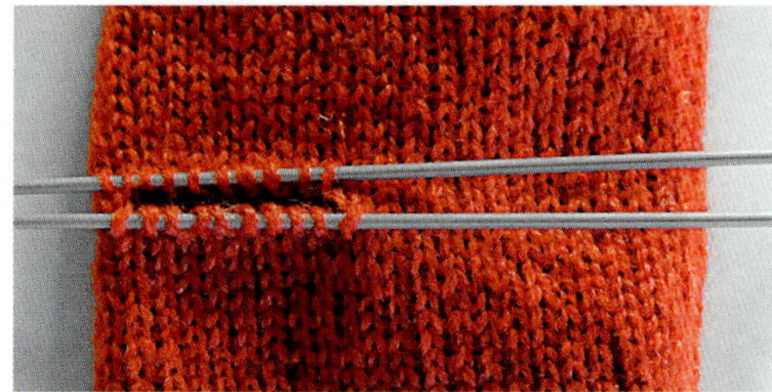

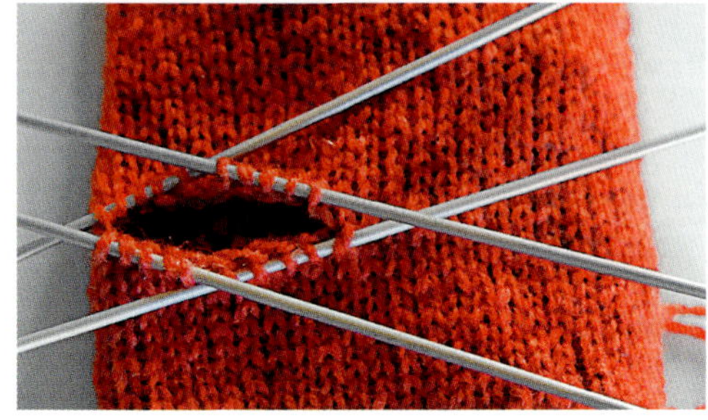

alpaca, machine-sewing is recommended. Make a multi-stitch zigzag with 2 lines on each side of the center steek stitch. For crochet reinforcement, check the internet for how-to videos.

Thumb: When the pattern instructions say to "set aside 15 stitches for the thumb," the easiest method is to knit the 15 stitches with

a smooth, contrast-color scrap yarn. Slide the stitches back to the left needle and work them in a single color or in pattern as shown on the chart.

When the mitten is finished, pick up the stitches above and below the scrap yarn. The pattern might say, for example, "pick up 17 +17 stitches for the thumb." Begin below the scrap yarn and insert a double-pointed needle through the loops. Always begin 1 stitch to the right of the scrap yarn to avoid a hole. Insert the needle from right to left, picking up the right half of each stitch until you have the correct number of stitches on the needle.

Cutting steeks on knitted garments: Before cutting a steek open, you should reinforce it with sewing or crochet so the work won't unravel. If you knitted with a woolen-spun pure, non-superwash wool yarn, you can reinforce with hand-sewing or crocheting through all the stitches. If your yarn is a smooth, worsted yarn, or a yarn blend with a fiber like

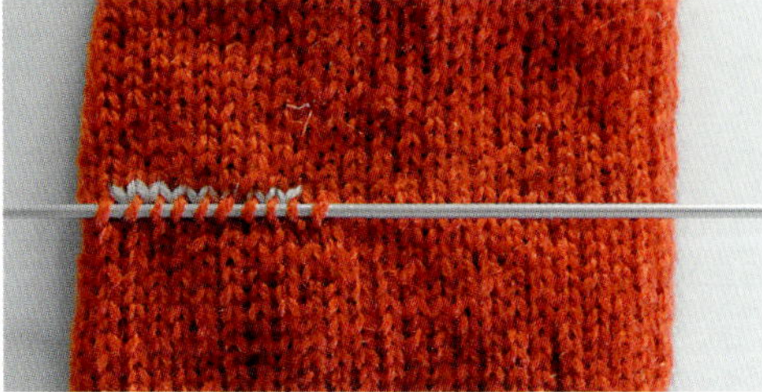

Turn the work and do the same thing on the upper set of stitches. Begin 1 stitch to the right of the scrap yarn and pick up the right half of each stitch until you have the correct number of stitches on the needle. Carefully remove the scrap yarn and divide the stitches onto four double-pointed needles.

If the upper and lower stitch counts don't match, move the thumb stitches to a holder or scrap yarn. When you come to the next round, increase to the correct number of stitches.

Yarn floats: If you leave long floats on the inside of your knitting, toes or fingers can easily catch on the loose strands. For patterns where the float is more than 5-6 stitches, I recommend that you twist the strands around each other on the wrong side. Be careful not to stack the twists, though—that will make them visible on the right side.

Two-end (twined) purl braid: Some of the socks in this book feature two-end braids (sometimes called Latvian or Estonian braids). The braid helps prevent a lower edge from rolling up. The yarn is held in front of the work as you form the braid. You'll need two colors for a braid, blue and white, for example.

To make a braid, work as follows:
Rnd 1: (K1 blue, k1 white) around.
Rnd 2: Bring both strands to the RS. Begin with blue and purl 1 over the previous blue stitch.

Keeping the blue on the RS, move it to the right, laying it OVER the white strand. *Now bring the white strand UNDER the blue and purl 1 over the previous white stitch. Move the white to the right and lay it OVER the blue strand.

Bring the blue strand UNDER the white and purl 1. Always work blue over blue and white over white. Move the blue to the right and lay it OVER the white.* Repeat from * to * around. End with p1 white. Throughout, the strand you pick up always comes UNDER the strand you just purled with.

As you work, the yarns will twist together. Just move the twist down and wait until the next round; once you reach more twists in the opposite direction, the yarns will straighten out again.

The second half of the chevron braid is formed by reversing the twisting of the yarns. Begin the next round with *purl 1 blue over the previous blue stitches. Keep the strand on the RS and to the right. Now bring the white yarn OVER the blue and purl 1. Move white to the right and beneath the blue on the RS. Bring the blue OVER the white, p1. Leave white on RS to the right and down.* Repeat from * to * around. End with p1 white. Throughout, the yarn to be used next comes OVER the previous strand.

If you've worked the second purl round correctly, the yarns will have untwisted by the end of the round.

Triangular Shawl with Crocheted Scallop Edge

Many old shawls are edged with crocheted scallops. The first traces of crochet work in Europe date to the first half of the nineteenth century—which is about the same time that thin cotton yarn came onto the market in large quantities. The introduction of spinning machines in the 1760s allowed for increased cotton production in America. The "spinning jenny" was one of the most important inventions of the Industrial Revolution.

When it first made its way to Scandinavia, crochet was a technique typically used by the upper class and was reserved for luxury work. In Denmark, the handcraft association, which was led by landed gentry, tried to keep farm women away from this "unnecessary and harmful handcraft." In the meantime, in Ireland, crocheted lace with fine cotton thread brought in valuable income, desperately necessary because the country was ravaged by hunger from 1845 to 1850. Here in Norway, we've found a number of crocheted pieces from the middle of the nineteenth century and later.

This garter stitch shawl is knitted with a fine Spelsau yarn and is especially warm, a pleasure to lay over your shoulders on a late summer evening—or on a nippy day in autumn. It has a crocheted scallop edge inspired by the old garter stitch shawls found in the Folkenborg Museum in Eidsberg in Østfold.

INSTRUCTIONS

Skill Level: Easy

FINISHED MEASUREMENTS
Length: approx. 102 in / 260 cm
Width: at widest point down center back,
27½ in / 70 cm

MATERIALS
Yarn:
CYCA #1 (fingering) Hoelfeldt Lund natural-
ly-dyed spelsau strikkegarn 2 tr—two-ply knitting yarn (100% wool, 244 yd/223 m / 50 g)

Yarn Colors and Amounts:
Gray: 400 g
Dark Gray: 100 g
OR
CYCA #2 (sport, baby) Hillesvåg ullvarefabrikk
Sol lamullgarn (100% lamb's wool, 317 yd/
290 m / 100 g)

Yarn Colors and Amounts:
Light Heather 58413: 350 g
Charcoal 58415: 100 g

Needles:
U. S. size 6 / 4 mm

Crochet Hook:
U. S. G-6 / 4 mm

GAUGE
20 sts x 17 garter ridges (= 34 knit rows) =
4 x 4 in / 10 x 10 cm.
Adjust needle size to obtain correct gauge if
necessary.

This shawl is knitted in garter stitch. It begins
at the top center back and is worked back and
forth, increasing at both the center and on
each side.

SHAWL
With Gray, CO 3 sts and knit back.
Row 1: Kb&f into 1st st (knit into back loop
as if for a twisted knit and then knit into front
loop as for a usual knit st and slip both sts off
needle), yo, k1, yo, k1 = 6 sts total.
Row 2: Kb&f into 1st st, knit to end of row.
Row 3: Kb&f into 1st st, k2, yo, k1, yo, k3 = 10
sts total. Pm around the center st between the
yarnovers and move marker up every row.
Row 4: Work as for Row 2 = 11 sts total.
Rep Rows 3-4. You will begin every row with
an increase. On every other row, you'll also
increase 2 sts at the center with yo, k1, yo.
In other words, on every rep of Row 3, you
increase 3 sts, and on every rep of Row 4, you
increase 1 st. Each rep of the two pattern rows
= 1 garter ridge.

When the shawl is about 19¾ in / 50 cm high,
change to Dark Gray. From this point on,
change colors every 1¼ in / 3 cm. After 3 dark
stripes, work 1 more light stripe (1¼ in / 3 cm
wide).

CROCHETED SCALLOP EDGING
With Gray, work 1 sc in each st/row all around
the shawl. Make scallops along long outer
edge: 1 sc, skip 1 sc, 5 dc in next sc, *skip next
sc, 1 sc, skip next sc, 5 dc in next sc*; rep * to *
across, working 7 dc at the tip of center back.

FINISHING
Weave in all ends neatly on WS. To even out
the scallops, block shawl by first gently washing
it in lukewarm water with wool-safe soap.
Squeeze out excess water and roll in a terrycloth towel to absorb more water. Pin out shawl
on blocking squares and leave until completely
dry. Alternatively, you can pin out the shawl
first, spritz it with lukewarm water, and leave it
until completely dry—at least 24 hours.

Roses from Asker

In my book *Socks from Around Norway*, I wrote about my inspiration for designing a pair of socks with a rose motif I found on my father-in-law's old ski stockings. I discovered them in a bag of assorted woolens that had been stored away. They were from a time when it was common to wear knickerbockers and patterned stockings for skiing, and they likely came from somewhere between World War II and the early 1950s.

I'm pretty sure the stockings were knitted by my husband's grandmother, Otilie Sæther, née Rønsen (1880-1964). She was originally from Eidsvoll, and came to Asker in 1905 when the Dikemark hospital was ready. She trained as a Red Cross sister and worked as a nurse, first in Dikemark and then at the Blakstad hospital.

The stockings were knitted with natural sheep's wool in black and white, and are slightly felted. The heel (a type of common heel seamed at the center of the sole) is quite worn and was darned with brown yarn. Someone also tried to repair the tips of the stockings.

The pattern is usually referred to as an "endless pattern," which means you can repeat the motif forever. For this book, I used the same rose motif for a hat and a pair of mittens. This time, I combined it with a lace pattern I found on an old pair of stockings. You can substitute regular ribbing for the lace if you prefer.

Rose Mittens from Asker

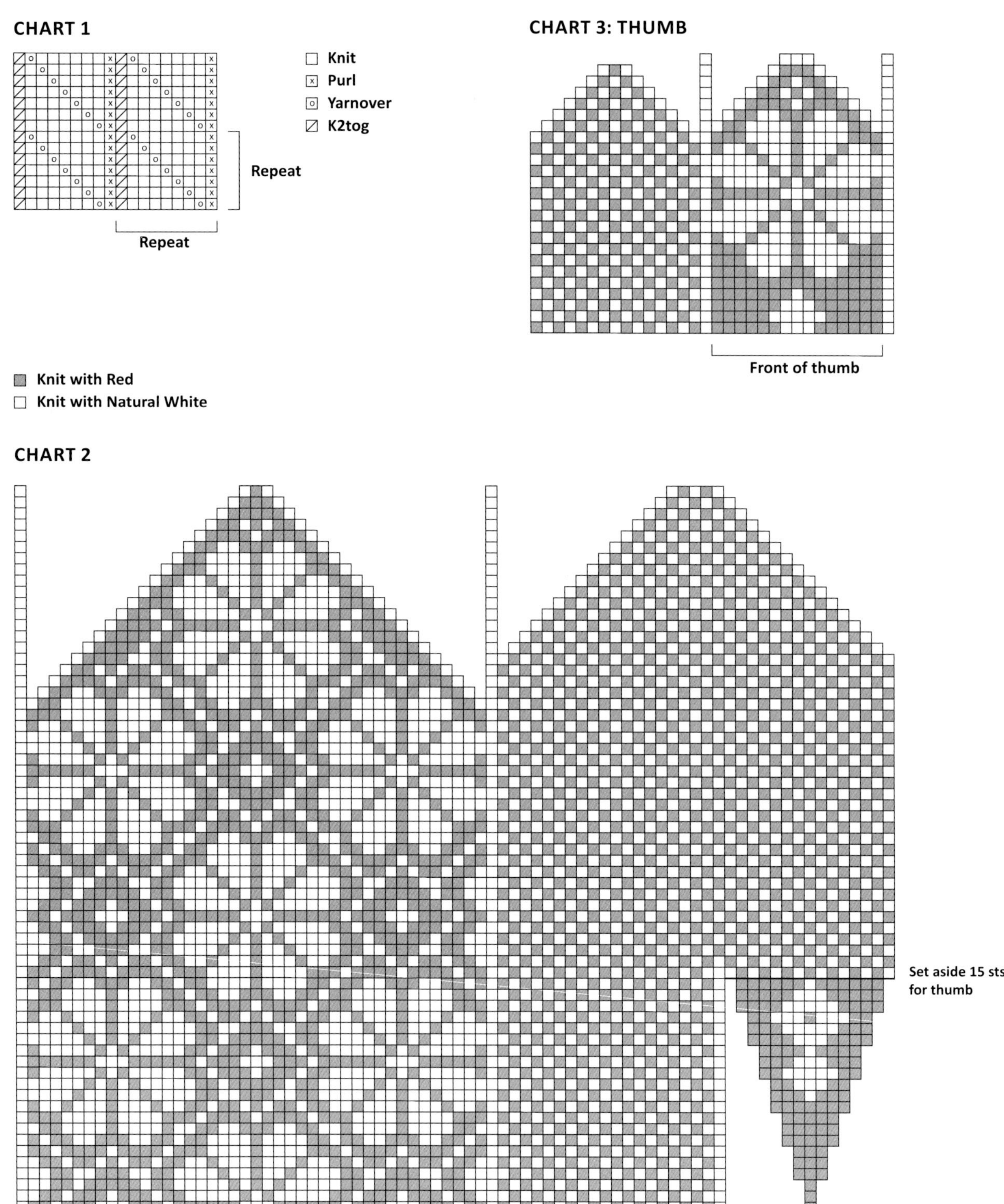

INSTRUCTIONS

Skill Level: Intermediate

SIZES
S (M)

MATERIALS
Yarn:
CYCA #1 (fingering) Hillesvåg ullvarefabrikk
Vilje lamullgarn (100% Norwegian lamb's wool,
410 yd/375 m / 100 g)

Yarn Colors and Amounts:
Red 57406: 50 g
Natural White 57400: 50 g

Needles:
U. S. size 0 (1.5) / 2 (2.5) mm: set of 5 dpn

GAUGE
The size is adjusted by changing the gauge/
needle size. Follow the same instructions for
both sizes.
Size S: 35 sts x 35 rnds = 4 x 4 in / 10 x 10 cm.
Size M: 32 sts x 34 rnds = 4 x 4 in / 10 x 10 cm.
Adjust needle size to obtain correct gauge if
necessary.

RIGHT MITTEN
With Red and dpn for chosen size, CO 72 sts.
Divide sts onto 4 dpn and join; pm for beginning of rnd. Knit 4 rnds. Turn work inside out.
Work following chart 1 or written instructions
below 2 times in length. The pattern shifts to
the right throughout so be careful to maintain
placement of beginning of rnd marker.

Lace Cuff Pattern
Rnd 1: *P1, yo, k6, k2tog*; rep * to * around.
Rnd 2: *P1, k1, yo, k5, k2tog*; rep * to * around.
Rnd 3: *P1, k2, yo, k4, k2tog*; rep * to * around.
Rnd 4: *P1, k3, yo, k3, k2tog*; rep * to * around.
Rnd 5: *P1, k4, yo, k2, k2tog*; rep * to * around.
Rnd 6: *P1, k5, yo, k1, k2tog*; rep * to * around.
Rnd 7: *P1, k6, yo, k2tog*; rep * to * around.

Continue until you have worked 6 rep of Rnds
1-7 and cuff measures approx. 3½ in / 9 cm.
Work 1 extra rnd without a yarnover so the rep
is 8 rather than 9 sts: *P1, k6, k2tog* = 64 sts
rem. Now work following Chart 2.

Increase for the thumb gusset as shown until
there are 15 gusset sts. See page 14 for thumbhole instructions. Continue following chart,
working top increases as shown. Cut yarn and
draw end through rem sts; tighten.

THUMB
Pick up and knit 16 + 16 sts = a total of 32 sts
around thumbhole (see page 14). Work around
in stockinette pattern, shaping thumb as shown
on Chart 3.

LEFT MITTEN
Work as for right mitten, reversing chart so
thumb is on left side of palm.

FINISHING
Weave in all ends neatly on WS. Gently
steam press mittens on WS under
damp pressing cloth.

Rose Hat from Asker

INSTRUCTIONS

Skill Level: Intermediate

SIZES
Head circumference: 22½ in / 57 cm
You can adjust the size by working on smaller needles (for smaller hat) or larger needles (for larger hat)

MATERIALS
Yarn:
CYCA #1 (fingering) Hillesvåg ullvarefabrikk Vilje lamullgarn (100% Norwegian lamb's wool, 410 yd/375 m / 100 g)

Yarn Colors and Amounts:
Red 57406: 50 g
Natural White 57400: 50 g

Needles:
U. S. size 1.5 / 2.5 mm: set of 5 dpn or short circular

GAUGE
32 sts x 34 rnds = 4 x 4 in / 10 x 10 cm.
Adjust needle size to obtain correct gauge if necessary.

HAT
With Red and short circular, CO 180 sts. Join, being careful not to twist cast-on row; pm for beginning of rnd. Knit 4 rnds. Turn work inside out. Work following Chart 1 (see page 22) or written instructions below. The pattern shifts to the right throughout, so be careful to maintain placement of beginning of rnd marker.

Lace Cuff Pattern
Rnd 1: *P1, yo, k6, k2tog*; rep * to * around.
Rnd 2: *P1, k1, yo, k5, k2tog*; rep * to * around.
Rnd 3: *P1, k2, yo, k4, k2tog*; rep * to * around.
Rnd 4: *P1, k3, yo, k3, k2tog*; rep * to * around.
Rnd 5: *P1, k4, yo, k2, k2tog*; rep * to * around.
Rnd 6: *P1, k5, yo, k1, k2tog*; rep * to * around.
Rnd 7: *P1, k6, yo, k2tog*; rep * to * around.

Rep Rnds 1-7 until brim measures approx. 3 in / 7.5 cm. Purl 3 rnds. On the last rnd, decrease 24 sts evenly spaced around to 156 sts. Now work following Chart 4; the 52-st pattern is repeated 3 times around. Shape top as shown on chart.

FINISHING
Weave in all ends neatly on WS. Gently steam press cap on WS under damp pressing cloth. Make a pompom about 2-2¾ in 5-7 cm in diameter and sew securely to top of hat.

Skaugum Rose Mittens

After Johann Gutenberg invented the art of book printing around 1450, many small printing companies were quickly established. Books and scriptures—for the most part with religious or scientific content—were printed. By 1520, the first textile pattern books saw the light of day. They were an immediate success all over Europe, among both professional handworkers and women who were responsible for the family's clothing and textiles.

The first known book of these patterns was published by Johann Schönsperger the Younger in 1523. *Ein Neu Modelbuch* [A New Pattern Book] was published in Augsburg, Germany with a combination of individual motifs and block patterns. It was well received, and the following year, some of the patterns were republished in a new book with the same name.

Its success was so big that several of Europe's leading printers decided to follow in Schönsperger's footsteps, and beginning in 1527, a number of books on embroidery and weaving were published in Germany, Italy, France, and the Netherlands. The designs were a mix of old and new, taken from local and more exotic sources.

These patterns must also have wandered northwards. Even if these early block patterns were originally meant for weaving, many of them could easily be converted into knit motifs. We've found these motifs used for knitted "night sweaters," of which we have so many examples in Scandinavian museum collections, but there are also other examples in our folk art tradition. Eight-petal roses and other flower motifs were included from the very beginning. It's easy to find yourself inspired by these old pattern books.

Skaugum, by the way, is near Asker, and is the official residence of Norway's Crown Prince Haakon and his family.

From Johann Siebmacher's Neues Modelbuch *[New Pattern Book], 1604.*

CHART 3: THUMB

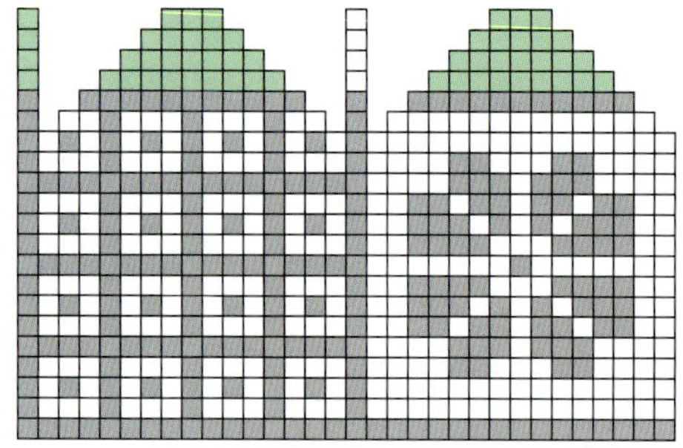

CHART 2

Set aside 14 sts
for thumb

CHART 1

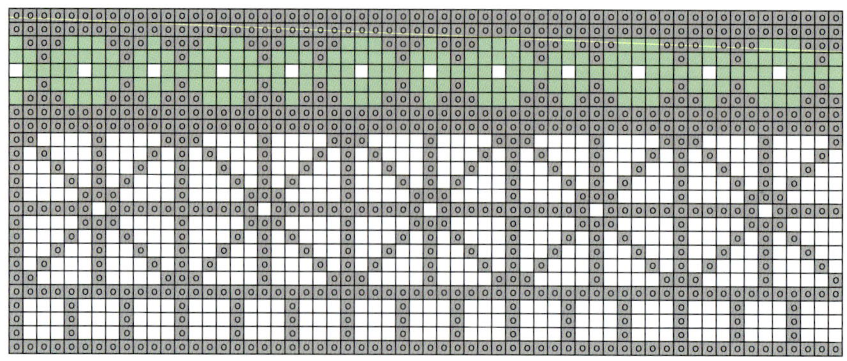

Color 1
Color 2
Color 3
Color 4

INSTRUCTIONS

Skill Level: Intermediate

SIZES
Women's

MATERIALS
Yarn:
The pattern uses four colors, but you could use two, three, or five colors. There are many spots where you could make a color change along the way. Use leftover yarns if you want.

CYCA #2 (sport, baby) Hillesvåg ullvarefabrikk Ask (Hifa 2) (100% Norwegian wool, 344 yd/315 m / 100 g)

Yarn Colors and Amounts:
Color 1: Dark Terracotta Red 316003: 50 g
Color 2: Light Pink 316121: 100 g
Color 3: Deep Rose Heather 316568: 50 g
Color 4: Bright Apple Green Heather 316588: 50 g
OR
CYCA #1 (fingering) Rauma Finull PT2 (100% Norwegian wool, 191 yd/175 m / 50 g)

Yarn Colors and Amounts:
Color 1: Terracotta 469: 50 g
Color 2: Light Pink 4686: 100 g
Color 3: Raspberry Red 456: 50 g
Color 4: Apple Green 455: 50 g

Other yarn options:
Rauma 2-ply Gammelserie (100% wool)
Du Store Alpakka Sterk

Needles:
U. S. size 1.5 / 2.5 mm: set of 5 dpn

GAUGE
28 sts x 32 rnds = 4 x 4 in / 10 x 10 cm. Adjust needle size to obtain correct gauge if necessary.

These mittens are knitted traditionally, from the bottom up. You can use a long magic loop circular, but the pattern is written for the traditional set of 5 dpn.

RIGHT MITTEN
With Color 2, CO 72 sts. Divide sts evenly onto 4 dpn and join; pm for beginning of rnd. Work the lace edging as follows:

Rnd 1: *K2tog, k4, yo, k4, k2tog tbl*; rep * to * around.
Rnd 2: Knit around.
Rnd 3: *K2tog, k3, yo, k1, yo, k3, k2tog tbl*; rep * to * around.
Rnd 4: K4, *k2tog tbl, k9*; rep * to * around, ending with k2tog tbl, k5.
Rnd 5: *K2tog, k2, yo, k1, yo, k1, yo, k2, k2tog tbl*; rep * to * around.
Rnd 6: K3, *k2tog tbl, k2tog tbl, k7*; rep * to * around, ending with k2tog tbl, k2tog tbl, k4.
Rnd 7: *K2tog, k1, yo, k1, yo, k1, yo, k1, yo, k1, k2tog tbl *; rep * to * around.
Rnd 8: K2, *k2tog tbl, k2tog tbl, k2tog tbl, k5*; rep * to * around, ending with k2tog tbl, k2tog tbl, k2tog tbl, k3.
Rnd 9: *K2tog, yo, k1, yo, k1, yo, k1, yo, k1, yo, k2tog tbl *; rep * to * around.
Rnd 10: Knit around = 66 sts rem.
Rnd 11: Decrease 6 sts evenly spaced around [= (k9, k2tog) around] = 60 sts rem.

Continue, following Chart 1. After completing cuff, change to Color 3 and work following Chart 2. Increase for the thumb gusset as shown until there are 14 gusset sts. See page 14 for thumbhole instructions (working sts onto scrap yarn). Continue following chart, working top decreases as shown. On the left side of the mittens, decrease with k2tog; on the right side, ssk or sl 1, k1, psso. When 8 sts rem, cut yarn and draw end through rem sts; tighten.

THUMB
Pick up and knit 16 + 16 sts = a total of 32 sts around thumbhole (see page 14). Work around in stockinette pattern, shaping thumb as shown on Chart 3. Decrease and fasten off as for top of mitten.

LEFT MITTEN
Work as for right mitten, reversing chart so thumb is on left side of palm.

FINISHING
Weave in all ends neatly on WS. To give your mittens a professional look, wash them gently in lukewarm water and wool-safe soap. Dry flat, pinning out lace points so they will look especially nice. Leave pinned until completely dry.

Small Party Bag

The Norwegian Folk Museum (Norsk Folkemuseum) has several small bags in its collections. Many of them are knitted in one lace pattern or another, and most are worked in cotton yarn. They're registered by the museum with various Norwegian words for "bag," including *pose*, *pung*, *portemoné*, and *pompadur*. Unfortunately, we seldom know their origin.

Thin cotton yarn became available in large quantities at the end of the eighteenth century. Steadily increasing cotton production in America and the development of spinning machines meant the use of cotton exploded. Between 1770 and 1780, England was consuming 5.7 million pounds / 2.6 million kilos a year of cotton textiles on average. Fifty years later, consumption had increased to 269 million pounds / 122 million kilos annually. The need for labor increased in step with the production explosion. By the time the American Civil War began in 1861, there were 2.5 million slaves working on cotton plantations in the South.

In Norway, the first cotton spinning mills were established at the beginning of the nineteenth century. Cotton was a new and exciting material that was quickly adopted by the upper class. Cotton was used for various types of lace knitting. Knitted lace edgings appeared on hats, along necklines, and on the lower edges of sleeves. Small bags were also knitted with cotton yarn.

Inspired by these handy little bags, I knitted a version in black fine wool yarn. A small dark bag of this type is a fine accessory for a dress or *bunad* (traditional Norwegian folk costume).

INSTRUCTIONS

Skill Level: Intermediate

FINISHED MEASUREMENTS
Length: approx. 9 in / 23 cm
Diameter: approx. 9¾ in / 25 cm

MATERIALS
Yarn:
CYCA #1 (fingering) Rauma Baby Panda (100% Merino wool, 191 yd/175 m / 50 g).
If you choose a different yarn and use a heavier yarn and larger needles, your bag will be bigger.

Yarn Color and Amount:
Black 36: 100 g

Needles:
U. S. size 1.5 / 2.5 mm: short circular and set of 5 dpn

GAUGE
36 sts = 4 in / 10 cm.
Adjust needle size to obtain correct gauge if necessary.

CO 180 sts. Join, being careful not to twist cast-on row; pm for beginning of rnd. Knit around for 1½ in / 4 cm. Purl 1 rnd for foldline. Now work in lace pattern described below, repeating pattern 8 times in length. Maintain marker at beginning of rnd; the pattern shifts to the right throughout.

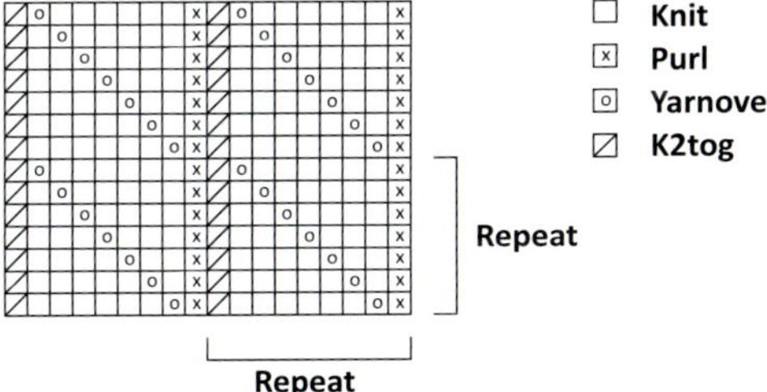

Rnd 1: *P1, yo, k6, k2tog*; rep * to * around.
Rnd 2: *P1, k1, yo, k5, k2tog*; rep * to * around.
Rnd 3: *P1, k2, yo, k4, k2tog*; rep * to * around.
Rnd 4: *P1, k3, yo, k3, k2tog*; rep * to * around.
Rnd 5: *P1, k4, yo, k2, k2tog*; rep * to * around.
Rnd 6: *P1, k5, yo, k1, k2tog*; rep * to * around.
Rnd 7: *P1, k6, yo, k2tog*; rep * to * around.
Rep Rnds 1-7 8 times.

Shape bottom:
Work Rnds 1-6. Work Rnd 7 as *p1, k6, k2tog*; rep * to * around= 1 st less per rep.

For the 10th pattern rep, work:
Rnd 1: *P1, yo, k5, k2tog*; rep * to * around.
Rnd 2: *P1, k1, yo, k4, k2tog*; rep * to * around
Rnd 3: *P1, k2, yo, k3, k2tog*; rep * to * around.
Rnd 4: *P1, k3, yo, k2, k2tog*; rep * to * around.
Rnd 5: *P1, k4, yo, k1, k2tog*; rep * to * around.
Rnd 6: *P1, k5, k2tog*; rep * to * around.

For the 11th pattern rep, work:
Rnd 1: *P1, yo, k4, k2tog*; rep * to * around.
Rnd 2: *P1, k1, yo, k3, k2tog*; rep * to * around
Rnd 3: *P1, k2, yo, k2, k2tog*; rep * to * around.
Rnd 4: *P1, k3, yo, k1, k2tog*; rep * to * around.
Rnd 5: *P1, k4, k2tog*; rep * to * around.

For the 12th pattern rep, work:
Rnd 1: *P1, yo, k3, k2tog*; rep * to * around.
Rnd 2: *P1, k1, yo, k2, k2tog*; rep * to * around
Rnd 3: *P1, k2, yo, k1, k2tog*; rep * to * around.
Rnd 4: *P1, k3, k2tog*; rep * to * around.

For the 13th pattern rep, work:
Rnd 1: *P1, yo, k2, k2tog*; rep * to * around.
Rnd 2: *P1, k1, yo, k1, k2tog*; rep * to * around
Rnd 3: *P1, k2, k2tog*; rep * to * around.

For the 14th pattern rep, work:
Rnd 1: *P1, yo, k1, k2tog*; rep * to * around.
Rnd 2: *P1, k1, k2tog*; rep * to * around.

End shaping with (p1, k2tog) around. Cut yarn and draw end through rem sts; tighten.

FINISHING
Weave in all ends neatly on WS. Turn facing at foldline and sew down facing on WS.
Knit two I-cords (see below), each about 20½ in / 52 cm long. Thread each cord halfway through the first row of lace above facing. Sew each cord end to end to make a ring. Fasten off well.

KNITTED I-CORD
With dpn, CO 4 sts. *Bring yarn from left side of needle and knit beginning at right side of needle; *at the same time*, tug on the yarn on WS.* Make sure RS is always facing you. Rep * to * until cord is desired length.

Beginner's Shawl

Christian Krohg's painting "Fight for Existence" (1889) was inspired by his observations of real life. The artist had seen with his own eyes bread passed out to the poor from a bakery at the corner of Skippergaten and Karl Johan in central Oslo. We are aware of a total of thirteen sketches working up to the final painting, which resides in Norway's National Museum, as well as two later versions and three copies.

The picture is a major work of realism; Krohg was concerned with showing what he considered a social problem under debate. In the breadline, we see women and children with outstretched arms in hope of getting something to eat on a cold winter day. In the background, we see a policeman who struts by, apparently content and unaffected. He can be regarded as a symbol of the official indifference to poverty.

We can also clearly see that the adult women in the picture are wearing shawls over their shoulders, crossed at the front and tied together at the back. This style of shawl had become extremely popular in the second half of the nineteenth century. They were easy to knit and affordable, and they could keep both the back and front of the upper body warm.

Shawls and scarves are also news these days, first and foremost as lovely, cozy accessories. The shawl I made here is easy to knit. You start at one point and gradually increase before decreasing at the same rate. The pattern's the same whether you use the yarn I suggest or another. Just make sure the yarn and needles suit each other.

INSTRUCTIONS

Skill Level: Easy

FINISHED MEASUREMENTS
Length: 85 in / 216 cm
Width: at widest point 19¾ in / 50 cm

MATERIALS
Yarn:
CYCA #1 (fingering) Hillesvåg Vilje lamullgarn (100% Norwegian lamb's wool, 410 yd/375 m / 100 g) or similar yarn

Yarn Color and Amount:
Astrid dyed by Ninapetrina: 200 g

Needles:
U. S. size 6 / 4 mm

GAUGE
20 sts x 42 rows (= 21 ridges) in garter st = 4 x 4 in / 10 x 10 cm.
Adjust needle size to obtain correct gauge if necessary.

SHAWL
The shawl is knitted back and forth in garter stitch.

CO 3 sts. Knit 6 rows. On the next row, increase 1 st by working kb&f into 1st st (knit into back loop as if for a twisted knit and then knit into front loop as for a usual knit st and slip both sts off needle). Rep this increase row on every 4th row until there are 100 sts.

Now knit 6 rows. On the next row, decrease instead of increasing, begin row with: sl 1, k1, psso. Knit to end of row. Decrease the same way on every 4th row until 3 sts rem. BO.

FINISHING
Weave in all ends neatly on WS. Block shawl by first gently washing it in lukewarm water with wool-safe soap. Squeeze out excess water and roll in a terrycloth bath towel to absorb more water. Pin out shawl on blocking squares and leave until completely dry— at least 24 hours.

Flower Mittens from Oslo

The Norwegian Folk Museum has a distinctive pair of mittens covered in flower motifs. There's no real certainty about their origin; the best guess is that they were made in Oslo, but even that isn't known for a fact. When people first began to collect items for museums, the emphasis was on describing and labeling the items themselves, rather than collecting information about their use or the user.

The original mittens were knitted on very fine needles in black and white yarn. The museum also has a similar pair with black roses on a white background. A pattern for a copy of these mittens is on page 32 of my book *Mittens from Around Norway*. Many knitters consider U. S. size 000 / 1.5 mm needles intimidatingly small. So I've reworked the pattern to allow it to be knitted with U. S. size 2.5 / 3 mm needles for the women's size and U.S. 4 / 3.5 mm for the men's. The ribbing has also been simplified. I've also designed a sock pattern with the same flowers.

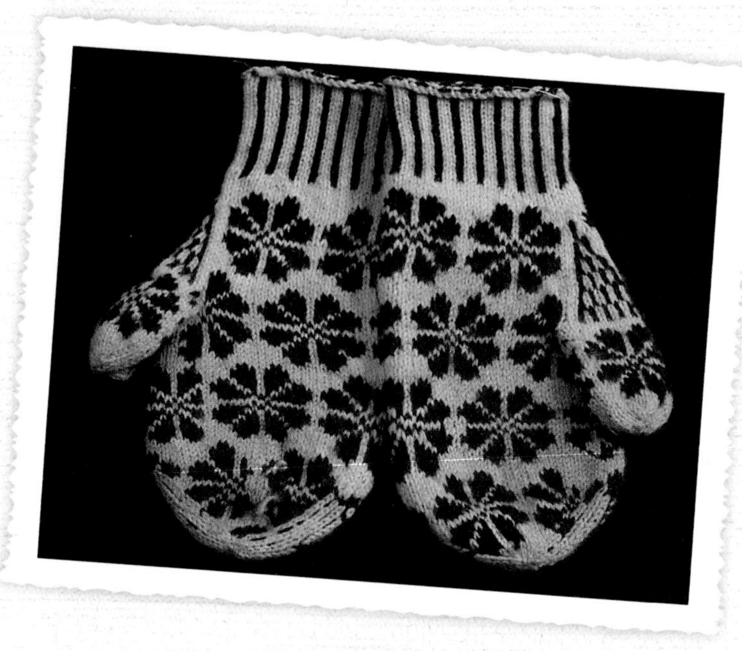

Flower Mittens

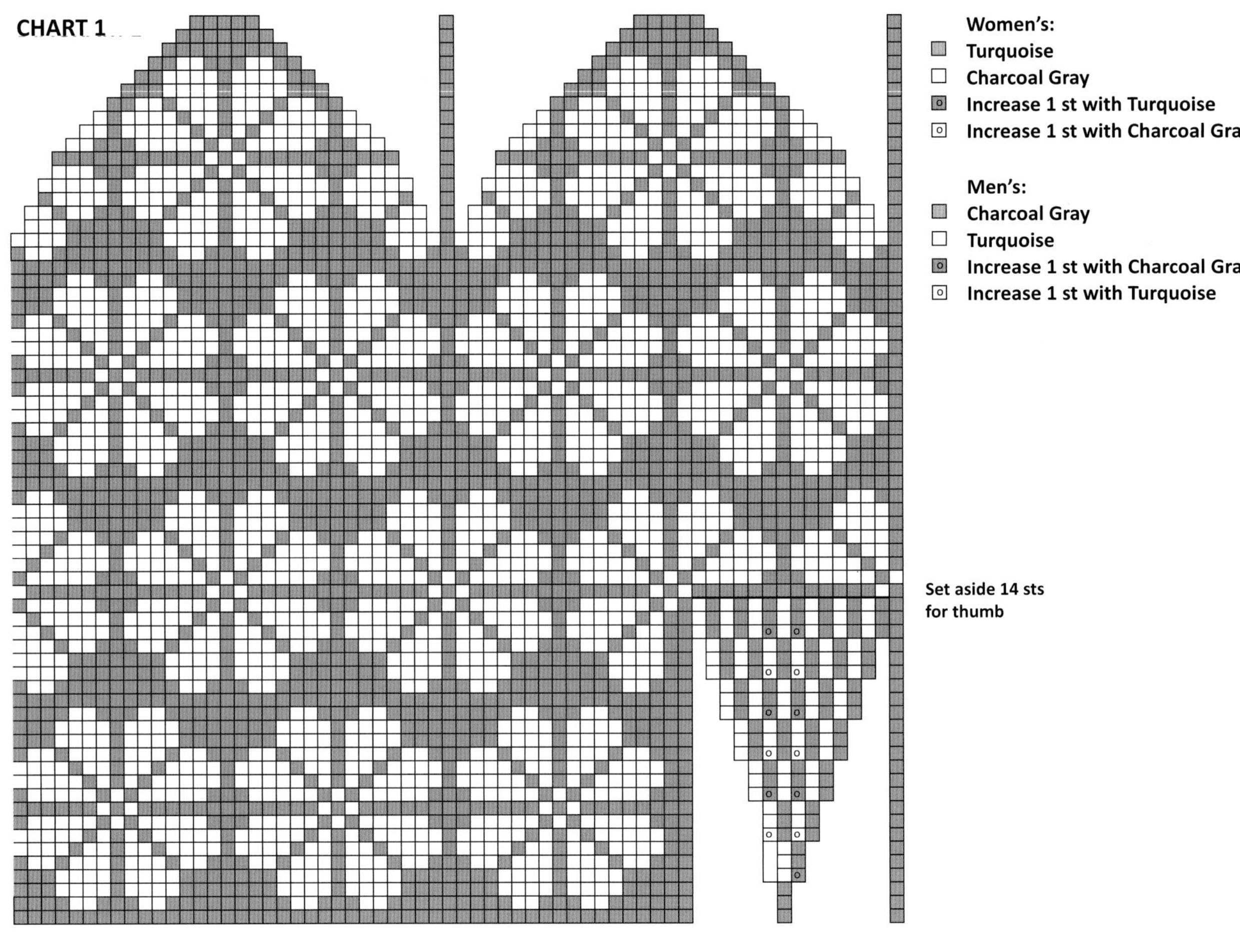

INSTRUCTIONS

Skill Level: Intermediate

SIZES
Women's (Men's)

MATERIALS
Yarn:
CYCA #2 (sport, baby) Hillesvåg ullvarefabrikk
Ask (Hifa 2) (100% Norwegian wool,
344 yd/315 m / 100 g)

Yarn Colors and Amounts:
Charcoal Gray 316056: 50 (100) g
Light Green Turquoise Heather 316584: 50
(100) g

Needles:
U. S. size 2.5 (4) / 3 (3.5) mm: set of 5 dpn

GAUGE
The size is adjusted by changing the gauge/
needle size. Follow the same instructions for
both sizes.

Women's: 26 sts x 28 rnds = 4 x 4 in /
10 x 10 cm.
Men's: 24 sts x 26 rnds = 4 x 4 in / 10 x 10 cm.
Adjust needle size to obtain correct gauge if
necessary.

RIBBING
With dpn for your size and Turquoise (Charcoal
Gray), CO 48 sts. Divide sts onto dpn and join.
Work 2 rnds k2, p2 ribbing. Change to the
opposite color—Charcoal Gray (Turquoise)—
and continue in k2, p2 ribbing until cuff measures 3¼ in / 8 cm.

RIGHT MITTEN
Continue in stockinette, following Chart 1, but
on the first rnd, increase 3 sts evenly spaced
around = 51 sts. Increase for the thumb gusset
as shown until there are 64 sts total (14 gusset
sts). See page 14 for thumbhole instructions
(working sts onto scrap yarn). Continue
following chart, working top increases as
shown. On the left side of the mitten,

CHART 2: THUMB

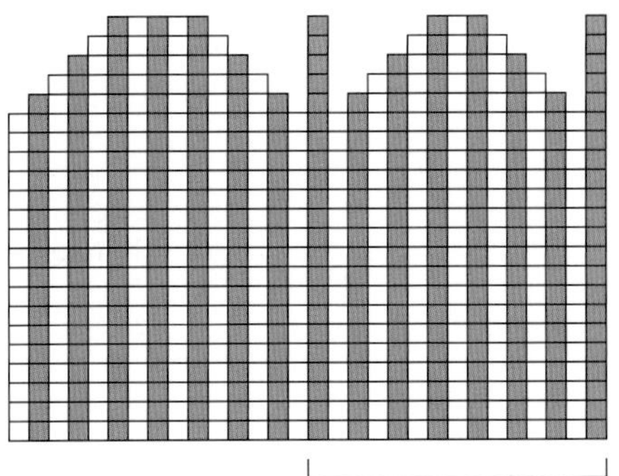

decrease with k2tog; on the right side, ssk or sl 1, k1, psso. When 12 sts rem, cut yarn and draw end through rem sts; tighten.

THUMB
Pick up and knit 15 + 15 sts—total of 30 sts around thumbhole (see page 14). Work around in stockinette pattern on Chart 2. Make sure stripes on thumb align with those on hand. Shape thumb tip as shown on chart. Decrease to 10 sts and fasten off as for top of mitten.

LEFT MITTEN
Work as for right mitten, reversing chart so thumb is on left side of palm.

FINISHING
Weave in all ends neatly on WS. Gently steam press mittens under a damp pressing cloth.

Flower Socks

Instructions on next page

CHART 4

CHART 3

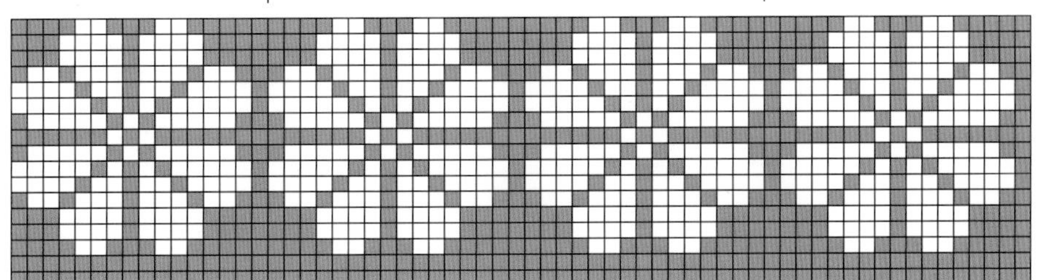

43

INSTRUCTIONS

Skill Level: Intermediate

SIZES
Women's (Men's)

MATERIALS
Yarn:
CYCA #1 (sport, baby) Du Store Alpakka Mini Sterk (100% Norwegian wool, 344 yd/315 m / 100 g)

Yarn Colors and Amounts:
Turquoise 834: 50 (50) g
Navy Blue 827: 50 (50) g
Light Blue 848: 50 (500) g

Needles:
U. S. size 1.5 (2.5) / 2.5 (3) mm: set of 5 dpn

GAUGE
32 (30) sts = 4 in / 10 cm.
Adjust needle size to obtain correct gauge if necessary.

LEG
With Turquoise and dpn for chosen size, CO 60 sts. Divide sts onto 4 dpn and join.
Rnd 1: *K2tog, k2, yo, k1, yo, k2, k2tog tbl, p1*; rep * to * around (each rep = 10 sts),
Rnd 2: *K9, p1*; rep * to * around.
Work Rnds 1-2 a total of 8 times.
Change to Navy and knit 1 rnd (= Rnd 1 of Chart 3), increasing 4 sts evenly spaced around = 64 sts. Work pattern following Chart 3 (see page 43).

COMMON HEEL
After completing sock leg, divide sts, placing 31 sts on a holder for instep (see chart).

Decrease 1 st at center back and work the heel flap back and forth over 2 dpn over the 32 sts at center back (place 16 sts on each needle). Begin with RS facing you.
Row 1: Change to Navy. Sl 1 pwise, knit to end of row.
Row 2: Change to Turquoise. Sl 1, purl to end of row.
Continuing with Turquoise only, rep Rows 1-2 until there are 12 chain sts at each side.
Turn heel:
Row 1: Sl 1. Knit until 5 sts rem on first dpn, k2tog, k3. K3 on next dpn, ssk, knit to end of row.

Row 2: Sl 1, purl to end of row.
Row 3: Sl 1. Knit until 4 sts rem on 1st dpn, k2tog, k2. K2 on next dpn, ssk, knit to end of row.
Row 4: Sl 1, purl to end of row.
Row 5: Sl 1. Knit until 3 sts rem on 1st dpn, k2tog, k1. K1 on next dpn, ssk, knit to end of row.
Row 6: Sl 1, purl to end of row.
Row 7: Sl 1. Knit until 2 sts rem on 1st dpn, k2tog. On next dpn, ssk, knit to end of row.
Row 8: Sl 1, purl to end of 1st dpn; yarn is at center of heel flap.
Hold the two needles with RS facing (=WS facing out on each). K2tog joining 1 st from each needle. *K2tog again, pass 1st st over 2nd. Continue from * until all sts have been bound off and 1 st loop rem.

Place held instep sts onto 2 dpn. Make sure RS faces you. Beginning at center of heel, with Navy and Ndl 1, pick up and knit 1 st in each chain st on side of flap. You can pick up the sts twisted or knit each through back loop to twist on following rnd. Work across instep in pattern with Ndls 2 and 3. With Ndl 4, pick up and knit 1 st in each chain st on side of flap. Knit the first st on Ndl 1 and move it to Ndl 4 = 64 sts total.

FOOT
Continue in stockinette pattern following Chart 4. Make sure flowers align and stack as shown. On last rnd, decrease 1 st at center of sole = 63 sts rem.

STAR TOE
Change to Turquoise and begin at center of sole. Work:
Decrease Rnd 1: *K5, k2tog*; rep * to * around. Knit 5 rnds.
Decrease Rnd 2: *K4, k2tog*; rep * to * around. Knit 4 rnds.
Decrease Rnd 3: *K3, k2tog*; rep * to * around. Knit 3 rnds.
Decrease Rnd 4: *K2, k2tog*; rep * to * around. Knit 2 rnds.
Decrease Rnd 5: *K1, k2tog*; rep * to * around. Knit 1 rnd.
Decrease Rnd 6: *K2tog*; rep * to * around.
Cut yarn and draw end through rem sts; tighten.

Make second sock the same way.

Shawl from Glomdalen

The Glomdalen Museum has a shawl purchased at a flea market in Elverum in about 1960 and later donated to the museum. I found a very similar shawl in Sørlandet. The look of this one is typical for the second half of the nineteenth century and beginning of the twentieth century, when knitted shawls and throws were common in all levels of society. This is a copy.

Lace was definitely popular among the upper classes at the beginning of the 1800s. Many young girls were sent to private schools to learn handwork skills, and knitted samples have been saved that show the various techniques they had to learn. One of the most impressive is a pattern strip in the Nordenfjeldske Kunstindustrimuseum (Nordenfjeld Art-Industry Museum) in Trondheim. It's 4¼ yd / 3.86 m long and about 2½ in / 6 cm wide. It has a total of 83 patterns on it, only five of which weren't a lace knitting in one form or another.

The National Museum in Oslo also has several knitted samples of the same type, and there are a couple more in the Norwegian Folk Museum. The pieces in the National Museum are all from the beginning of the nineteenth century. These cotton samplers are worked with precision, carefully mounted on paper, and edged with a yellow-gold handwoven tabby weave silk ribbon.

Silhouette of Miss or Mrs. Cappelen from 1897 or earlier.

INSTRUCTIONS

Skill Level: Adventurous Beginner

FINISHED MEASUREMENTS
Length: 56¾ in / 144 cm
Width: at widest point at center, 23¾ in / 60 cm

MATERIALS
Yarn:
CYCA #1 (fingering) Rauma 2-ply Gammelserie
(100% Norwegian wool, 175 yd/160 m / 50 g)
OR
CYCA #1 (fingering) Rauma Finull PT2 (100% Nor-
wegian wool, 191 yd/175 m / 50 g)

Yarn Color and Amount:
Natural White 401: 200 g

Needles:
U. S. size 2.5 / 3 mm: long circular

GAUGE
21 sts x 46 rows (= 23 ridges) = 4 x 4 in /
10 x 10 cm.
Adjust needle size to obtain correct gauge if
necessary.

Most of this shawl is knitted in garter stitch, but
it also has a couple of lace panels. You begin at
the top, at center back, and knit back and forth,
increasing at both the center and at each side. The
lace edging is worked separately and sewn to the
shawl in finishing.

SHAWL
CO 3 sts and knit 1 row.
Row 1: Kb&f into 1st st (knit into back loop as if for
a twisted knit and then knit into front loop as for a
regular knit st and slip both sts off needle), yo, k1,
yo, k1 = 6 sts total.
Row 2: Kb&f into 1st st, knit to end of row = 7 sts.
Row 3: Kb&f into 1st st, k2, yo, k1 (center st, pm
around st), yo, k3 = 10 sts.
Row 4: Work as for Row 2 = 11 sts.
Continue as est. You increase 1 st at the beginning
of every row. On every other row, you increase 2 sts
at the center—you'll have 3 new sts on odd-numbered rows, and 1 new st on even-numbered rows.

Rows 1-2 = 1 ridge.

When there are 65 sts and piece measures approx.
14¼ in / 36 cm long (down center back), change to
lace pattern, continuing increases as est:

Row 1: Kb&f into 1st st, *yo, k2tog* rep * to * until
1 st before center st, yo, k1, yo, work (k2tog, yo) to
end of row.
Row 2: Kb&f into 1st st, knit to end of row.
Rep these 2 rows 13 times.

Change back to garter st ridges as before until there
are 13 ridges = 364 sts total. BO loosely.

LACE EDGING
CO 16 sts and knit 1 row.
Row 1: K1, yo, (k2tog) 5 times, yo, k2tog, yo, k2tog,
yo, k1.
Row 2: Kb&f into 1st st, k5, p5, k2.
Row 3: K2tog, yo, k5, yo, (k2tog, yo) 3 times, k1.
Row 4: Kb&f into 1st st, k7, p5, k2.
Row 5: K2tog, yo, k5, yo, (k2tog, yo) 4 times, k1.
Row 6: Kb&f into 1st st, k9, p5, k2.
Row 7: K2tog, yo, (k1, yo) 5 times, (k2tog, yo) 5
times, k1.
Row 8: Kb&f into 1st st, k22.
Row 9: K2, pass 1st st over 2nd, k1, pass previous st
over. Continue binding off until you've bound off 8
sts and 1 st rem on right needle and 15 sts on left
needle, yo, (k2tog) 5 times, yo, k2tog, yo, k2tog, yo,
k1.

Rep Rows 2-9 until edging reaches all around shawl
long edge. Make sure you ease it in well over the
center back point with an extra lace point. Finish on
Row 9 and BO rem sts.

FINISHING
Weave in all ends neatly on WS. Fold lace edging
in half to find center. Pin edging to edge of shawl.
Make sure edging has plenty of ease at the tip so it
lies smoothly. Sew edging to shawl. Begin at the tip
at center—sew down one side and then the other.

To keep the edging neat, the shawl should be
stretched and pin-blocked. Lay it on a blocking mat,
foam board or something similar. You can wash the
shawl in lukewarm water and wool-safe soap first.
Gently squeeze out excess water and then roll in
a terrycloth towel to remove more water. Pin out
shawl. Or you can pin the shawl to the board first
and spritz it with lukewarm water. In either case,
leave shawl pinned out until completely dry—at
least 24 hours.

Striped Shawl from Øyer

Several shawls with characteristic striped edgings have been preserved in Øyer in Gudbrandsdalen. One such shawl (*bundingstørkle*) was, along with numerous other items, registered in 1984 as part of the Norwegian Handcraft Association's and the Norwegian Folk Museum's traveling exhibition "Knitting Then and Now."

The inner section of this shawl is a single color, black, while the outer part has black and white stripes—almost like the keys on a piano. The outer striped section is edged with a twisted black and white crochet chain cord. The neckline of the single-color part is edged with crocheted picots.

The shawl belonged to Helga Andersgård, born in Holen in 1905. She took the shawl with her to Fossegården when she married in 1936.

Inspired by Helga's shawl and its striped edge, I made a soft, pretty version in pink and gray lamb's wool yarn. If you want to make a similar shawl to go with your *bunad* (folk costume), you can choose other colors, heavier yarn, and larger needles, and follow the same instructions.

INSTRUCTIONS

Skill Level: Adventurous Beginner

FINISHED MEASUREMENTS
Length: 50½ in / 128 cm
Width: at widest point at center (before blocking), 25¼ in / 64 cm

MATERIALS
Yarn:
CYCA #1 (light fingering) Rauma Røros Lammullgarn (100% Norwegian lamb's wool, 273 yd/250 m / 50 g)

Yarn Colors and Amounts:
Pink L84: 100 g
Gray L12: 50 g

Needles:
U. S. size 2.5 / 3 mm: long circular

Crochet Hook:
U. S. size D-3 / 3 mm

GAUGE
26 sts x 50 rows (= 25 ridges) = 4 x 4 in /
10 x 10 cm.
Adjust needle size to obtain correct gauge if necessary. If you knit more tightly, the shawl will be smaller; if you knit more loosely, it will be larger.

This shawl is worked in garter stitch in two sections. You begin at the top, at center back, and knit back and forth, increasing at both the center and each side. The striped edging is worked separately and sewn on in finishing.

SINGLE-COLOR SECTION
With Pink, CO 3 sts. Knit 1 row.
Row 1: Kb&f into 1st st (knit into back loop as if for a twisted knit and then knit into front loop as for a regular knit st and slip both sts off needle), yo, k1, yo, k1 = 6 sts total.
Row 2: Kb&f into 1st st, knit to end of row = 7 sts.
Row 3: Kb&f into 1st st, k2, yo, k1 (center st, pm around st), yo, k3 = 10 sts.
Row 4: Work as for Row 2 = 11 sts.
Continue as est. You increase 1 st at the beginning of every row. On every other row, you increase 2 sts at the center, so, you will have 3 new sts on odd-numbered rows and 1 new st on even-numbered rows.

Rows 1-2 = 1 ridge.
When there are 75 sts and piece measures approx. 15¾ in / 40 cm down center back, BO and set piece aside while you knit striped edging.

STRIPED EDGING
With Pink, CO 5 sts. *Increase on the next row with kb&f into the first st; knit to end of row. Turn and knit back*. Rep * to * until you have 3 pink ridges (+ the cast-on row); change to Gray and knit 2 ridges, increasing as est. The color change should occur at the non-diagonal edge. Continue to work 3 Pink and 2 Gray ridges (= 1 repeat) *at the same time* as you increase to a total of 35 sts. Now continue without increasing until you've completed 32 repeats total. Change to Pink, knit until 1 st rem; turn and knit back. On the next row, knit until 2 sts rem; turn and knit back. Don't forget to maintain stripe sequence. Continue the same way until 4 sts rem, knitting 1 st more before each turn. At the point, there should be 3 Pink ridges (5 sts, 4 sts, 5 sts). Continue the same way until you once again have 35 sts on the needle. Now work the second half as for the first. On the last section, decrease on the inside instead of increasing. Decrease at beginning of row with sl 1, k1, psso. Continue as est until 5 sts rem. BO.

CROCHETED BAND
Crochet one Pink and one Gray chain stitch band, each long enough to surround outer edge of shawl + a little extra. Do not cut yarn; that way, you can lengthen the chain easily if necessary. Make corresponding chains for the line between the Pink and striped sections.

FINISHING
Sew the single-color and striped sections together. Loosely twist two crocheted chains together (one strand of each color) and, *at the same time*, sew down along striped edge with about one stitch every ⅜ in / 1 cm. Make sure the cord is long enough. Sew down the other twisted cord between the striped and Pink sections.

Weave in all ends neatly on WS. Gently wash shawl in lukewarm water and wool-safe soap. Roll shawl in a terrycloth towel to remove excess water. Pin out shawl on blocking mats or foam board, stretching out evenly to measurements. Leave shawl pinned out until completely dry—at least 24 hours.

Children's Mittens from Valdres

The Norwegian Institute for Bunad and Folk Costumes has registered a pair of light blue and white children's mittens from Sør-Aurdal in Valdres. They are knitted with fine, soft wool yarn; there's a charming little panel on the bottom of the cuff, and the twisted ribbing above the panel means the mittens fit snugly around the wrists. This pattern is easy and can be adapted for larger sizes.

INSTRUCTIONS

Skill Level: Intermediate

SIZES
6 (8, 10) years

MATERIALS
Yarn:
CYCA #3 (DK, light worsted) Sjølingstad Uldvare-fabrik / Vest-Agder Museum 3-ply Sjølingstad-garn (100% Norwegian wool, 251 yd/230 m / 100 g)

Yarn Colors and Amounts:
Sky Blue 212: 50 (50, 50) g
Natural White: 50 (50, 50) g

Alternate colors:
Light Petroleum 211, Orange 121, Pink 175

Needles:
U. S. size 2.5 / 3 mm: set of 5 dpn

GAUGE
24 sts x 30 rnds = 4 x 4 in / 10 x 10 cm.
Adjust needle size to obtain correct gauge if necessary.

RIGHT MITTEN
With White, CO 42 (48, 54) sts. Divide sts over 4 dpn and join; pm for beginning of rnd. Knit 3 rnds.
Eyelet Rnd (foldline): (K2tog, yo) around.
Now work in pattern following Chart 1. On the last rnd, decrease evenly spaced around to 34 (40, 46) sts. Work around in k1tbl, p1 ribbing until mitten is 3¼ in / 8 cm above foldline.

Continue in stockinette for 12 (14, 16) rnds and then set aside 7 (8, 9) sts at right side of palm for thumb (see page 14). Continue until mitten covers little finger (about 16 (18, 20) rnds.

Top Shaping:
Make sure you have the same number of sts on each needle.
X*Ndl 1: K1, sl 1, k1, psso. Knit until 3 sts rem on Ndl 2, k2tog, k1.* Rep * to * on Ndls 3 and 4.
Knit 1 rnd without decreasing.X
Rep X–X a total of 3 times.
Now decrease on every rnd (= rep * to *).
When 2 sts rem on each needle, cut yarn and draw end through rem sts; tighten.

THUMB
With Blue, pick up 9 (10, 11) + 9 (10, 11) sts = 18 (20, 22) sts total (see page 14). Divide sts onto 4 dpn and work around in stockinette. On 2nd rnd, k2tog at each side to avoid holes = 16 (18, 20) sts rem. Continue in stockinette until thumb is long enough, approx. 9 (10, 11) more rnds. Shape tip as for top of mitten, working X-X 2 times, and then cut yarn, draw end through rem sts; tighten.

LEFT MITTEN
Work as for right mitten, placing thumb at left side of palm.

FINISHING
Weave in all ends neatly on WS. Fold bottom of cuff along eyelet rnd and sew edge down on WS. Gently steam press mittens under a damp pressing cloth.

CHART 1

☐ White
▨ Sky Blue

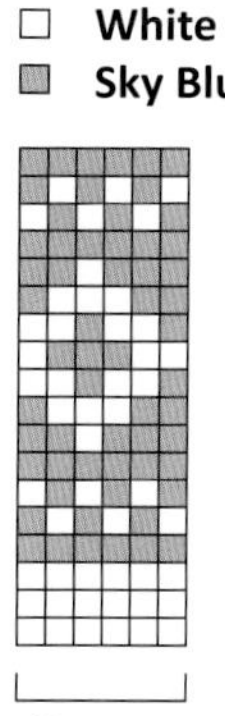

Repeat

Fishermen's Sweater from Drammen

In 1919, 123 portraits—18 of women and 105 of men—were found in the desk of district governor Theodor Christian Stoud Platou in Buskerud. The photos showed people from Drammen and the surrounding area who had been imprisoned for various crimes between 1866 and 1872 and had been held in the district jail in Hokksund. The women had been imprisoned for theft or morality violations, and the men for drunkenness and disorder, theft, fraud, or embezzlement. Some had also been violent and threatening.

As visiting card photographers became more and more common in the 1860s, the police began photographing criminals. The purpose was primarily to identify prisoners. However, these weren't "mugshots" as we know them today; they are confusingly similar to photos taken of regular people in photography studios, and most likely this style of photo was introduced by the police. The subject of the photograph sat on a chair at a little table and looked directly at the camera. In the background we can see drapes. In most of the photos, the subject's right hand is on the table, while the left hand is on the chair's arm or in the person's lap. These pictures are especially interesting because they show the type of clothing working people wore. Here we see patched skirts and trousers, worn-out jackets and gaping shoe soles. The outfits differ from the clothing styles of the solid middle class during the same time period.

Several of those shown in these photographs were wearing knitted garments. One of them was Edvart Gulliksen from Drammen, who was arrested for theft in 1868. Under his jacket, he was wearing a dark pullover of the same type commonly worn by seamen. Such sweaters, with knit and purl patterns, were produced for sale on the British Channel Islands and all along the eastern seaboard of England, and in the Netherlands. It is difficult to say whether the same type of sweater was also produced in Norway. Perhaps Edvart Gulliksen had been at sea, and got the sweater elsewhere before he was arrested?

Edvart Gulliksen, 1868.

Typically, these fishermen's sweaters were dark blue and called Guernseys or Channel Island pullovers. I chose a dark grey for my version. The pattern was designed the same way as the original sweaters.

INSTRUCTIONS

Skill Level: Experienced

SIZES
S (M, L, XL, XXL)

FINISHED MEASUREMENTS
Chest: 38½ (41, 43¾, 45¾, 48) in / 98 (104, 110, 116, 122) cm
Sleeve Length: 16¼ (16½, 17, 17¼, 17¾) in / 41 (42, 43, 44, 45) cm
Total Length: 22¾ (23¾, 24½, 25¼, 26) in / 58 (60, 62, 64, 66) cm

MATERIALS
Yarn:
CYCA #3 (DK, light worsted) Dale Garn Lanolin Wool (100% pure new wool, 109 yd/100 m / 50 g)

Yarn Color and Amounts:
Dark Gray Heather 1419: 550 (600, 650, 650, 700) g

Needles:
U. S. sizes 4 and 6 / 3.5 and 4 mm: short and long circulars + sets of 5 dpn; cable needle

GAUGE
21 sts x 30 rnds on larger needles = 4 x 4 in / 10 x 10 cm.
Adjust needle size to obtain correct gauge if necessary.

BODY
With larger circular, CO 195 (210, 220, 230, 245) sts. Join, being careful not to twist cast-on row; pm for beginning of rnd. Work ribbing as follows:
Rnd 1: *K3, p2*; rep * to * around.
Rnd 2: *K1, p1, k1, p2*; rep * to * around.
Rep Rnds 1-2 until ribbing measures 2 in / 5 cm. On the last rnd, increase/decrease evenly spaced around to 196 (208, 220, 232, 244) sts.

Pm at each side with 98 (104, 110, 116, 122) sts each for front and back.
K98 (104, 110, 116, 122), M1, k98 (104, 110, 116, 122), M1.
Rnd 1: K98 (104, 110, 116, 122), p1, k98 (104, 110, 116, 122), p1.
Rnd 2: Knit around.
Rep Rnds 1-2 and, *at the same time*, M1 on each side of each side st every 25th row twice.

Work new sts in garter st = 4 new sts per increase rnd and a total of 206 (218, 230, 242, 254) sts. Continue without further shaping until body measures 10¼ (10¾, 11, 11½, 11¾) in / 26 (27, 28, 29, 30) cm. Knit 1 rnd, decreasing 1 st each on front and back.

Now work charted pattern as follows.
Front: K1 (garter st), begin chart at arrow for your size and work 98 (104, 110, 116, 122) sts following chart, end at arrow for your size, k1 (garter st). Work back the same way.
　　When body measures 15¾ (16¼, 16½, 17, 17¼) in / 40 (41, 142, 43, 44) cm, BO 7 sts centered at each side for armholes (the garter st and 3 sts on each side of it). The body is divided so you now work back and forth on the back and front separately. When body measures 19 (19¾, 20½, 21¼, 22) in / 48 (50, 52, 54, 56) cm on the front and 19¾ (20½, 21¼, 22, 22¾) in / 50 (52, 54, 56, 58) cm on the back, shape neck as shown on the chart).

When front and back each measure 21¼ (22, 22¾, 23¾, 24½) in / 54 (56, 58, 60, 62) cm, place the 21 (23, 25, 27, 29) rem shoulder sts on a holder.

SHOULDERS AND SLEEVES
The shoulders each begin with a cable panel worked back and forth over the shoulder and then sts are picked up and knitted for the sleeve which is also worked back and forth, from the top down. Slip the first st on right shoulder (both front and back) onto a circular. Begin and end at neck. Hold the body with the front neck facing you, and CO 16 sts on right tip of circular; turn and k4, p8, k4. Turn.
Row 1 (RS): Sl 1, knit until 1 st rem. K2tog with 1 of the newly cast-on sts + 1 st from back, k1; turn.
Row 2 WS): Sl 1, k4, p8, k3, k2tog (1 newly cast-on st + 1 st from front), k1, turn.
Continue as est until you have worked 6 rows total.
Row 7: With RS facing, cross cable (= sl 1, k3, slip next 4 sts to cable needle and hold in front, k4, k4 from cable needle), k3, k2tog, k1; turn.
Row 8: Work as for Row 2.
Continue as est until all sts for the shoulder have been eliminated, *at the same time* crossing cable on every 8th row. End with Row 2.

When all the shoulder sts have been eliminated, pick up and knit 38 (40, 42, 44, 46) sts on each side of shoulder, using a crochet hook to make it easier = 94 (98, 102, 106, 110) sts total.

With RS facing, begin at underarm:

Row 1: Sl 1, knit across; turn.

Row 2: Sl 1, k42 (44, 46, 48, 50), p8, k43 (45, 47, 49, 51); turn.

Row 3: Work as for Row 1.

Row 4: Work as for Row 2.

Row 5: You will decrease on underarm and cross cable on this row. Sl 1, sl 1, k1, psso (= sl st just before knit st), k40 (42, 44, 46, 48), cross cable (= slip next 4 sts to cable needle and hold in front, k4, k4 from cable needle), knit until 3 sts rem, k2tog, k1; turn.

Row 6: Sl 1, p36 (38, 40, 42, 44), k5, p8, k5, p37 (39, 41, 43, 45); turn.

Continue as est with garter ridges and cables, following chart. *At the same time,* decrease 1 st on each side on the same row as cable crossing. The repeat for the ridges is over 6 rows, while you cross the cable on every 8th row. When sleeve measures 14¼ 14½, 15, 15½, 15¾ in / 36 (37, 38, 39, 40) cm, decrease evenly spaced across to 40 (45, 45, 50, 50) sts. Change to smaller dpn, join, and work ribbing as for lower edge of body for 2 in / 5 cm. BO in ribbing.

Make the second sleeve the same way.

NECKBAND

With smaller circular, pick up and knit a multiple of 5 sts all around neckline. Work ribbing as for lower edge of body for 2 in / 5 cm. BO in ribbing.

FINISHING

Seam underarms. Weave in all ends neatly on WS. Gently steam press pullover on WS under a damp pressing cloth.

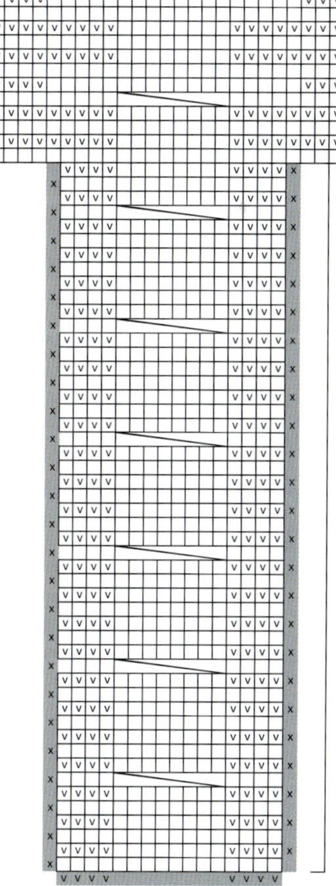

☐ Knit on RS
Ⅴ Purl on RS, knit on WS
▨ Shoulder on body
☒ K2tog with 1 st from shoulder on body and 1 st from shoulder strap
◹ Cross cable

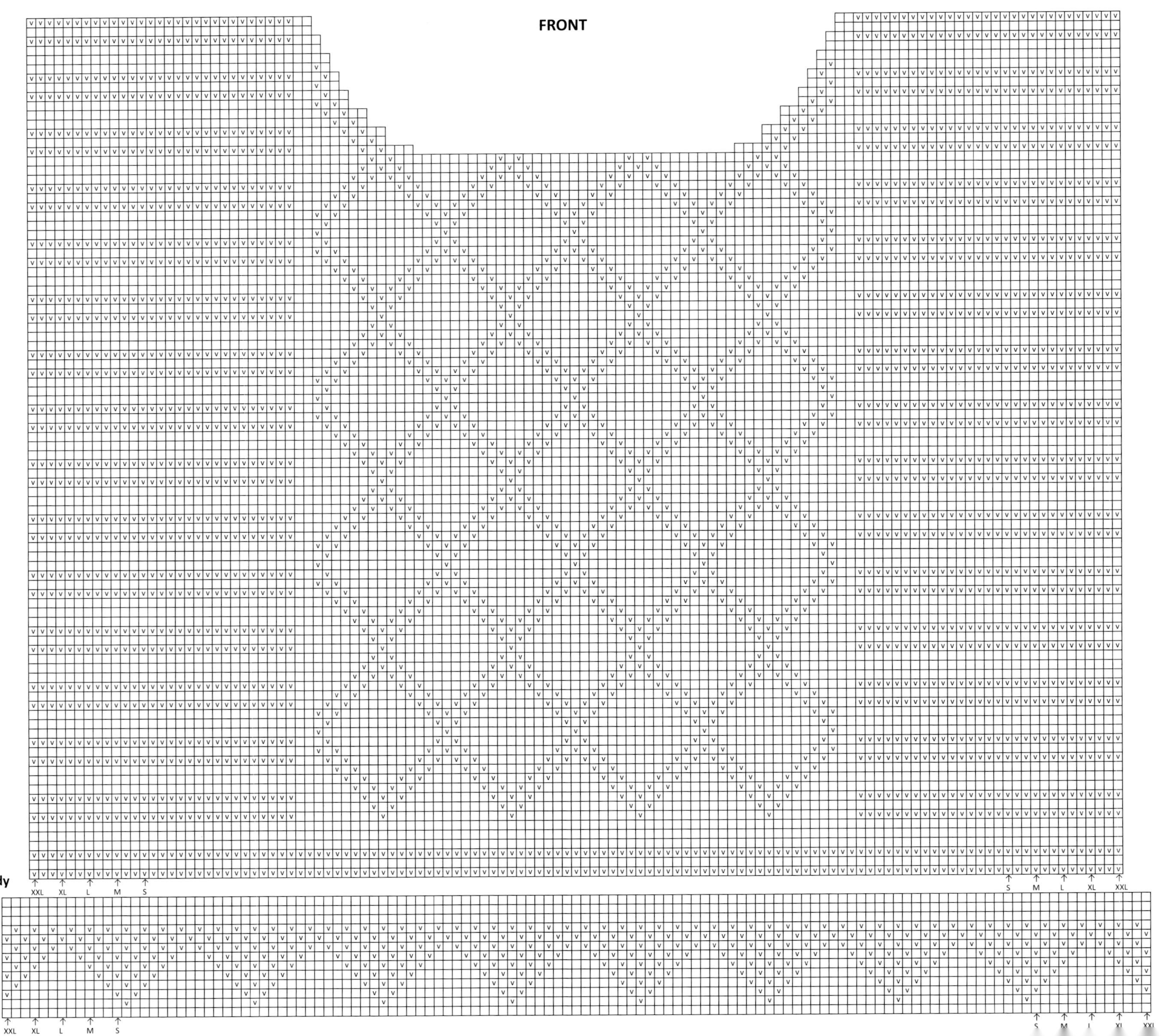

FRONT
62
Divide body
XXL XL L M S
S M L XL XXL
XXL XL L M S
S M L XL XXL

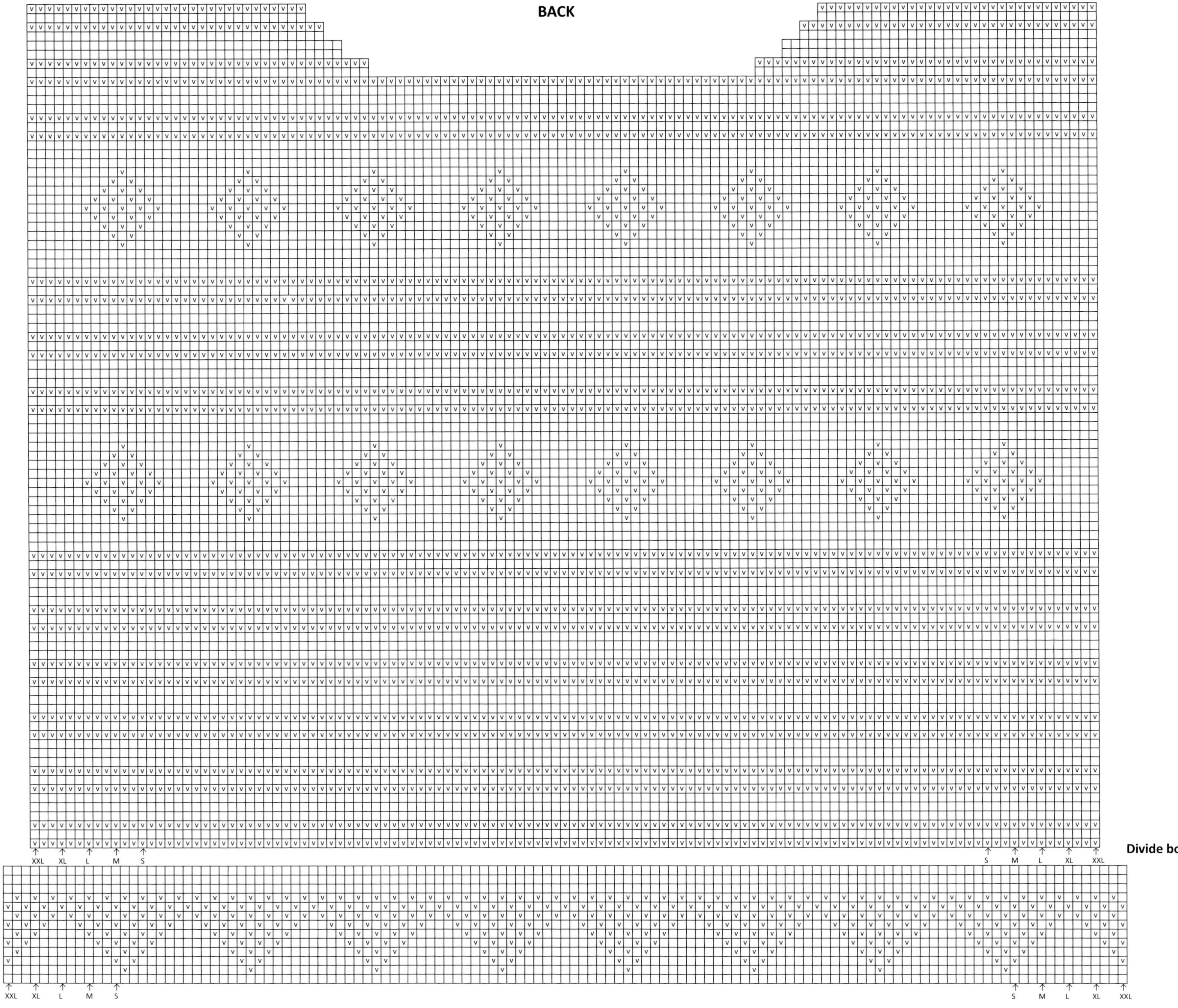

BACK
63
XXL XL L M S
S M L XL XXL
Divide body
XXL XL L M S
S M L XL XXL

Mittens from Lågendalen

Lågendalen is a valley in Norway that stretches from Larvik and Vestfold in the south, up along Numedalslågen, and then continues north to Kongsberg in Buskerud. The area north of Kongsberg is still a valley, but that one is called Numedal. The Lågdal Museum is just a few minutes away from the center of Kongsberg. There you'll find a simple mitten, possibly a child's, with a block pattern worked in sheep's wool, white and black. This pattern, with a cross in alternate blocks, is known all over southern Norway. I decided to play with the pattern a bit. The cuff is surrounded by flowers, and in the middle of the hand, I knitted in a bee. If you don't want the bee, you can fill the space with blocks instead. The thumb has three distinct hearts.

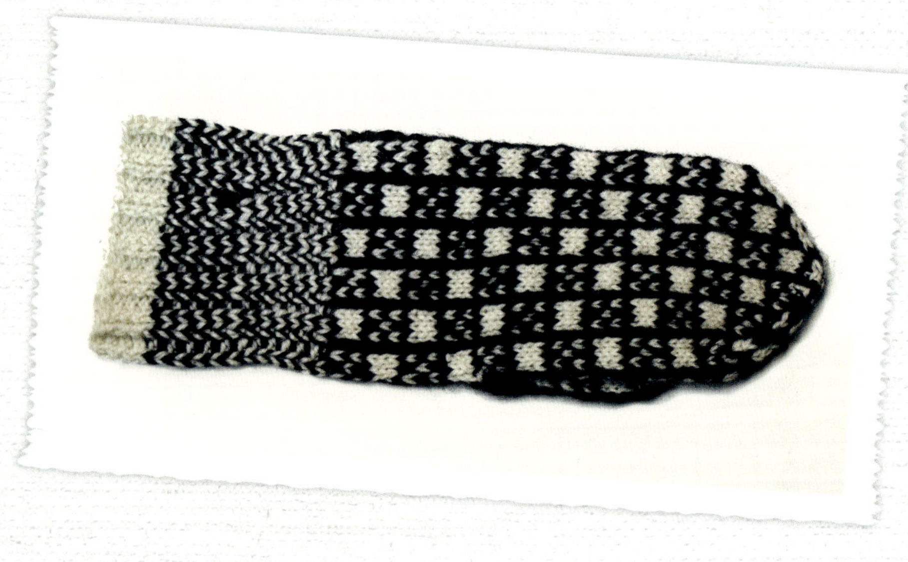

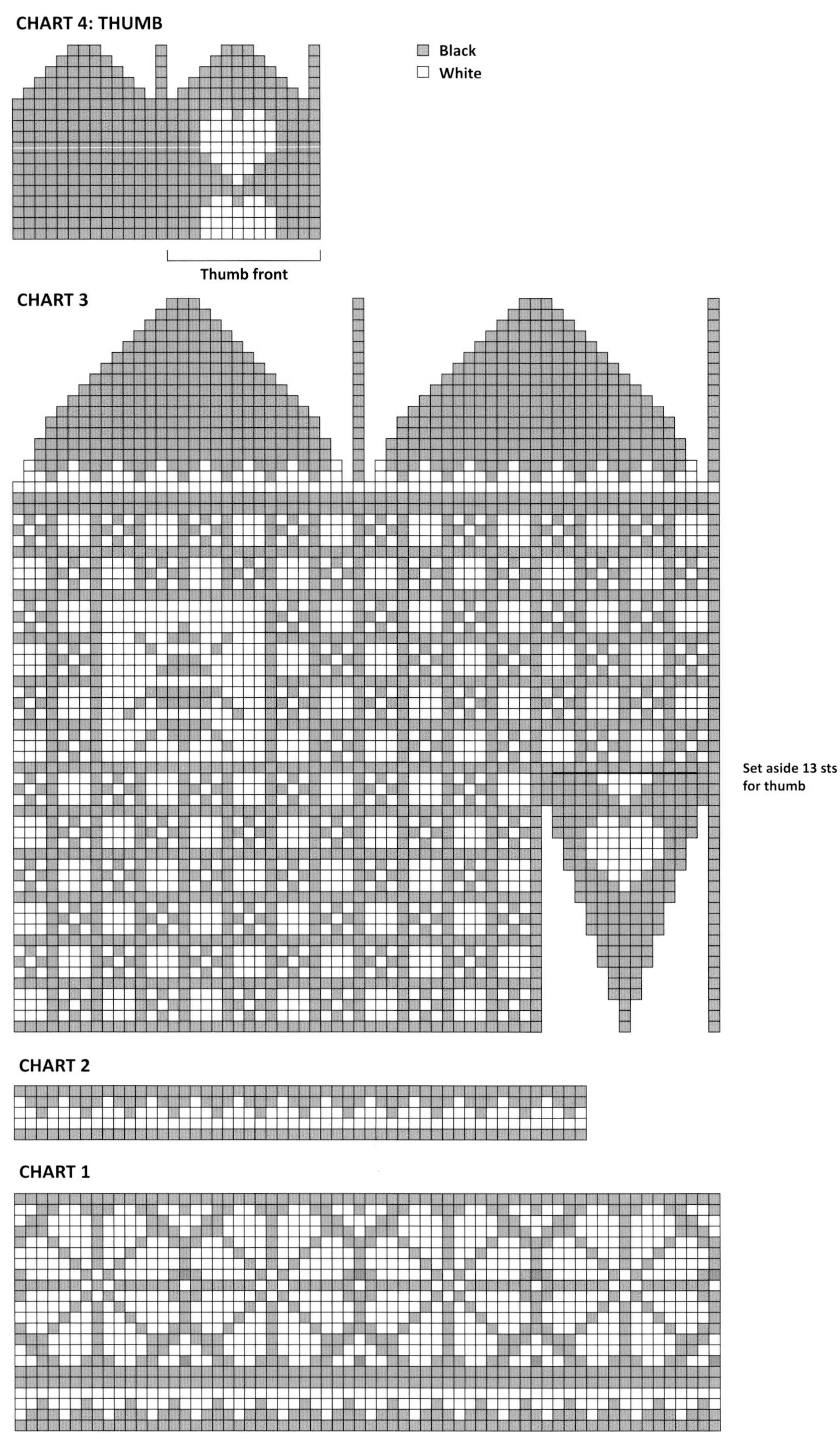

CHART 4: THUMB
Black
White
Thumb front
CHART 3
Set aside 13 sts
for thumb
CHART 2
CHART 1

INSTRUCTIONS

Skill Level: Intermediate

SIZE
Women's medium

FINISHED MEASUREMENTS
Length: 11¾ in / 30 cm
Width: across hand, 4¼ in / 11 cm
If you want to knit men's mittens with the same pattern, choose a slightly heavier yarn and needles U. S. size 4 or 6 / 3.5 or 4 mm. Follow the same instructions. You'll also need somewhat more yarn.

MATERIALS
Yarn:
CYCA #1 (fingering) Rauma Finull PT2 (100% Norwegian wool, 191 yd/175 m / 50 g)
OR
CYCA #3 (DK, light worsted) Du Store Alpakka Sterk (40% alpaca, 40% wool, 20% nylon, 150 yd/137 m / 50 g)

Yarn Colors and Amounts:
Finull PT2
Black 436: 50 g
Yellow 450: 50 g
OR
Sterk
Black 809: 50 g
Yellow 855: 50 g

Needles:
U. S. size 2.5 / 3 mm: set of 5 dpn

GAUGE
28 sts x 28 rnds = 4 x 4 in / 10 x 10 cm.
Adjust needle size to obtain correct gauge if necessary.

CUFF
With Black, CO 64 sts. Divide sts onto 4 dpn and join; pm for beginning of rnd. Knit 4 rnds and then purl 1 rnd (foldline). Now work following Chart 1. After completing charted rows, decrease evenly spaced around to 52 sts, being careful not to decrease in the center sts of a flower. Work following Chart 2. On the last rnd, decrease another 2 sts = 50 sts rem.

RIGHT MITTEN
Your mittens will look best if you place the center of the thumb gusset on the center st of a flower. Make sure the decreases don't interfere with this alignment.

Continue in stockinette and pattern and increase for thumb gusset as shown on Chart 3. Increase as shown until you have a total of 64 sts. Set aside 13 sts for thumb (see page 14). Continue in stockinette and pattern following chart. When shaping mitten top, k2tog on left side and sl 1, k1, psso on left side. When 8 sts rem, cut yarn and draw end through rem sts; tighten.

THUMB
With dpn (see page 14), pick up 14 + 14 sts = 28 sts total. Divide sts onto 4 dpn and work around in stockinette following Chart 4. Continue in stockinette and shape tip as for top of mitten. When 8 sts rem, cut yarn and draw end through rem sts; tighten.

LEFT MITTEN
Work as for right mitten, placing thumb at left side of palm and reversing charts to correspond.

FINISHING
Weave in all ends neatly on WS. Fold bottom of cuff along purl foldline and sew edge down on WS. Gently steam press mittens under a damp pressing cloth.

Small Party Bag from Vestfold

A number of small knitted pouches and party bags have been preserved. Many of them were knitted with cotton yarn, which became popular with the upper classes at the end of the eighteenth century; the trend spreading to all levels of society during the nineteenth century. Lace patterns of all sorts became very popular. The most elegant bags had intricate patterns that used beads, which had to be threaded onto the yarn before knitting.

Larvik Museum has a little bag in its collection that could be characterized as a work bag or project bag. Perhaps it was handy to have a little project bag to take along when visiting friends and neighbors? The bag was knitted in wool yarn in several colors, shading from dark to light. It was knitted in a typical wave pattern with vertical purl stripes. The top of the bag is ribbed with eyelet holes for threading a cord. Chenille tassels adorn the ends of the cord. The wave pattern is repeated at the very top. A similar bag could very easily be useful these days.

INSTRUCTIONS

Skill Level: Intermediate

FINISHED MEASUREMENTS
Width: 8¾ in / 22 cm
Length: 8¾ in / 22 cm

MATERIALS
Yarn:
CYCA #0 (lace) Anzula Cloud (80% Merino wool, 10% nylon, 10% cashmere, 575 yd/526 m / 114 g)

You can substitute another yarn but just make sure the yarn and needle size produce the fabric you want. If you choose a heavier yarn, the bag will be larger; a finer yarn will make a smaller bag.

Yarn Color and Amount:
Raspberry (hand-dyed): 100 g

Needles:
U. S. size 2.5 / 3 mm

Notions:
zipper 8¾ in / 22 cm long
optional: lining fabric to fit bag

GAUGE
25 sts x 32 rnds = 4 x 4 in / 10 x 10 cm.
Adjust needle size to obtain correct gauge if necessary.

BAG
NOTE: Hold yarn double throughout.
CO 112 sts. Join, being careful not to twist cast-on row; pm for beginning of rnd. Work around in Seafoam pattern (see below). One repeat is 11 + 3 sts which is worked 8 times around.

Rnd 1: *K11, p3*; rep * to * around.
Rnd 2: Work as for Rnd 1.
Rnd 3: *K2tog tbl, k2tog tbl, (yo, k1) 3 times, yo, k2tog, k2tog, p3*; rep * to * around.
Rnd 4: Purl.
Rep Rnds 1-4 until bag is same length as width (it will stretch a bit when blocked).
Slip 5 sts to right needle without knitting them, turn work so RS faces RS, and join bottom with 3-needle bind-off. Make sure the patterns align as you bind off. Hold the needles parallel. K2tog, joining 1st st of each needle. *K2tog again with next 2 sts. Pass 1st st on right needle over 2nd.* Rep from * to * until all sts have been bound off.

HANDLE
CO 11 sts and work back and forth in pattern:
Row 1: K11.
Row 2: P11.
Row 3: K2tog tbl, k2tog tbl, (yo, k1) 3 times, yo, k2tog, k2tog.
Row 4: K11.
Rep Rows 1-4 until handle is 19¾ in / 50 cm or 47¼ / 120 cm long, or desired length.

FINISHING
Weave in all ends neatly on WS. Block bag on a blocking matt or foam board. Pin out bag so the lace opens up well in all directions. Spray with clean water so it's thoroughly dampened. Leave until completely dry (at least 24 hours). Block the handle the same way. Sew in zipper by hand, about ¾ in / 2 cm in from the top edge. Attach handle at each side. Line bag if you want.

Woad Socks

Obtaining a blue dye has always been difficult. For that reason, blue yarn was expensive and blue was considered a status symbol. A box with woad seeds in it was found in the Oseberg ship, a well-preserved Viking ship discovered essentially intact inside a burial mound in Norway; that could indicate that the plant was cultivated in Viking times. Throughout the Middle Ages, woad was the most important source of blue coloration. Once trade was established with India, the discovery of indigo there led to serious competition for woad, as indigo produces an even more vibrant blue. Today, synthetic indigo is used for blue.

Woad is a plant in the cruciferous family. It can grow to a height of 15¾ to 59 in / 40 to 150 cm, and has yellow flowers. In Norway, it spread all the way up to Finnmark (far north). The Indian indigo plant has never been able to grow here, but some dyers are now experimenting with Japanese indigo.

Variations of the motif in these socks, which I've called Woad Socks, are found on garments all around Norway—on a pair of mittens from Lågendalen or Hallingdal, a sweater from Nordfjord, a pair of socks from Rogaland, even on filler used as insulation in Åmli. Flowers are among the oldest knitted motif we know. By the 1100s, they already appeared on various household textiles.

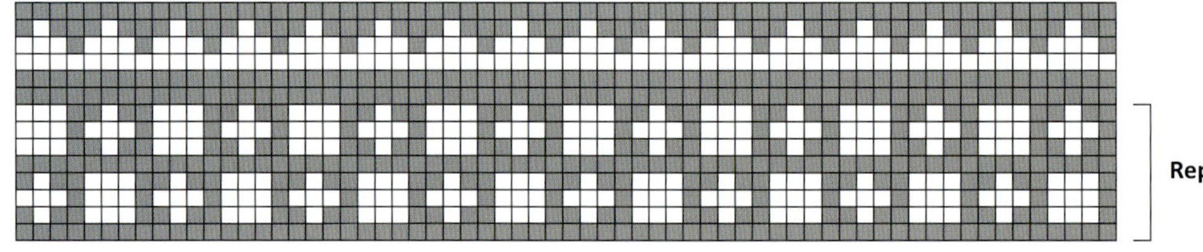

CHART 2
Repeat

CHART 1
Natural White
Blue

INSTRUCTIONS

Skill Level: Intermediate

SIZE
Women's medium
If you want to knit men's size socks with the same pattern, choose a slightly heavier yarn and needles U. S. size 4 or 6 / 3.5 or 4 mm. Follow the same instructions. You'll also need somewhat more yarn.

MATERIALS
Yarn:
CYCA #3 (DK, light worsted) Du Store Alpakka Sterk (40% alpaca, 40% wool, 20% nylon, 150 yd/137 m / 50 g)

Yarn Colors and Amounts:
Natural White 806: 50 g
Blue 815: 50g

Needles:
U. S. size 2.5 / 3 mm: set of 5 dpn

GAUGE
25 sts = 4 in / 10 cm.
Adjust needle size to obtain correct gauge if necessary. If you knit more loosely, the socks will be larger—and you'll need more yarn to complete them. If you knit more tightly, the socks will be smaller.

LEG
With Blue, CO 64 sts. Divide sts onto 4 dpn and join; pm for beginning of rnd. Knit 4 rnds and then purl 1 rnd. Work in stockinette pattern following Chart 1.

COMMON HEEL
After completing Chart 1/sock leg, divide the stitches, placing 32 sts on a holder for instep. These sts will rest until the heel is finished.

Heel Flap
Divide the rem 32 sts onto two dpn (= 16 sts per dpn) and work back and forth with Blue only.
Begin with the RS facing you.
Row 1 (RS): Sl 1 purlwise wyb, k31.
Row 2: Sl 1 purlwise wyf, p 31.
Repeat these 2 rows until there are 12 chain sts at each side of the flap.

Shaping the Heel
Now you will shape the back by decreasing as follows:
Row 1: Sl 1, knit until 5 sts rem on Ndl 1, k2tog, k3. On Ndl 2, k3, ssk, knit to end of needle.
Row 2: Sl 1, purl to end of row.
Row 3: Sl 1, knit until 4 sts rem on Ndl 1, k2tog, k2.

On Ndl 2, k2, ssk, knit to end of needle.
Row 4: Sl 1, purl to end of row.
Row 5: Sl 1, knit until 3 sts rem on Ndl 1, k2tog, k1. On Ndl 2, k1, ssk, knit to end of needle.
Row 6: Sl 1, purl to end of row.
Row 7: Sl 1, knit until 2 sts rem on Ndl 1, k2tog. On Ndl 2, ssk, knit to end of needle.
Row 8: Sl 1, purl to end of Ndl 2. Yarn is now at center of heel flap.
Hold the two dpn with RS facing in (so WS faces out on each side). Join the sets of sts with 3-needle BO: K2tog with 1 st from each needle, *k2tog with next st from each needle, pass first st over the second*. Repeat from * to * until 1 st loop rem.

FOOT
Divide the instep sts onto 2 dpn. With RS facing, with Blue, on Ndl 1, beginning at the center of the sole, knit to flap and then pick up and knit 1 st in each chain st on the side of the flap = total of 16 sts. You can pick up the chain sts through back loops or knit them tbl on the next rnd. Work the instep sts on Ndls 2-3 in pattern following Chart 2 (this rnd = Row 1 on Chart 2). With Ndl 4, pick up and knit 16 sts on opposite side of heel flap = 64 sts total. K2tog on last rnd = 63 sts total.

Continue in pattern following Chart 2. Work the repeat a total of 4 or 5 times, or until foot is desired length before toe (about 2 in / 5 cm before total foot length), ending with top motif on chart. K2tog on last rnd = 63 sts total.

STAR TOE
Begin at the center of the sole, with Blue.
Rnd 1: *K5, k2tog*; rep * to * to end of rnd.
Rnds 2-6: Knit.
Rnd 7: *K4, k2tog*; rep * to * around.
Rnds 8-11: Knit.
Rnd 12: K3, k2tog*; rep * to * around.
Rnds 13-15: Knit
Rnd 16: K2, k2tog*; rep * to * around.
Rnds 17-18: Knit.
Rnd 19: K1, k2tog*; rep * to * around.
Rnd 20: Knit.
Rnd 21: K2tog*; rep * to * around.

FINISHING
Cut yarn and draw end through rem sts; tighten. Weave in all ends neatly on WS. Make the second sock the same way. Gently steam press socks under a damp pressing cloth to block.

Minister's Mittens

This photograph of the clergyman Harald Olsen Kaldor (1882-1953), out skiing in his minister's garb and white ruff collar after a service, fascinates me. Usually we see photos or portraits of serious-looking ministers who are either sitting or standing. It's winter, clearly snowy and cold—and we see a clergyman on skis, presumably for the trip to and from the church. Perhaps it's his wife Anne Othilie Lindstad (born in 1890) behind him?

The photo is from Møsstrond Church in Rauland, in Vinje. The church is on the little island of Hovden in Møsvatn, 2,953 feet / 900 meters above sea level. This mountain village is still without a road. The photo must have been taken between 1923, when the church was finished, and 1927, when Kaldor became the parish minister in Romedel on Hedemark.

Ruff collars of various sizes and shapes were a fashionable accessory for women and men in the European upper classes between 1550 and 1650. The constricted collar edges on shirts gradually become larger and more encompassing. A ruff collar is a round collar with its white linen formed into folds—ruffs. It must be stiff and shaped with a pipe iron, and it was a big job to make. Even after the ruff collar went out of style, it continued to be a part of clerical dress for several centuries. In Norway, the white ruff collar was worn together with a black cassock up until 1981, when the clothing of Norwegian clergy was simplified, but both Danish and Icelandic ministers continue to wear ruff collars.

In the photo, we see the minister is also wearing rounded-top mittens with a simple pattern of triangles. Since the cuffs aren't visible, I allowed myself to embellish them with a star panel.

Harald Olsen Kaldor on skis at Møsstrond Church.

CHART 4: WOMEN'S THUMB

CHART 4: MEN'S THUMB

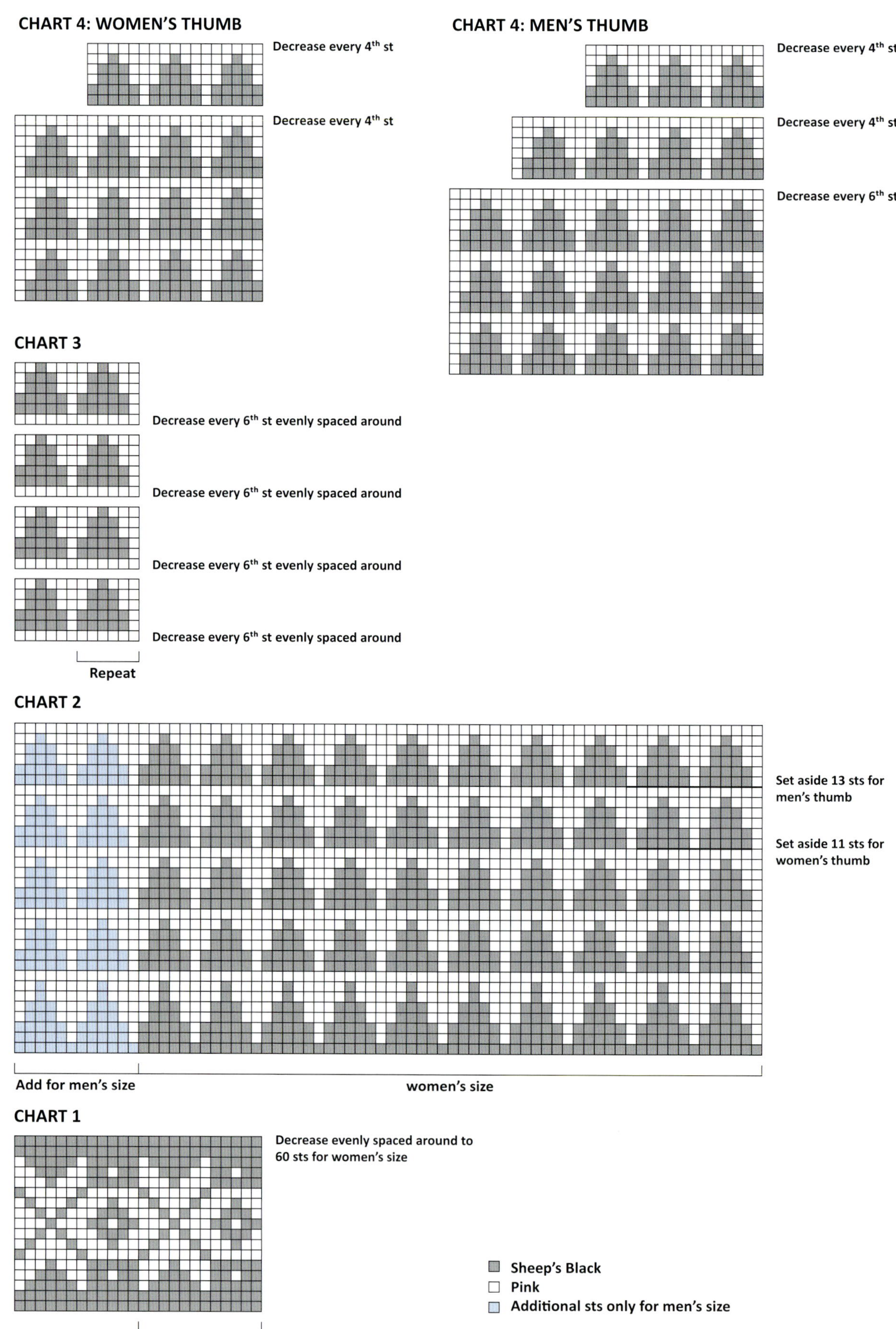

INSTRUCTIONS

Skill Level: Intermediate

SIZES
Women's (Men's)

MATERIALS
Yarn:
CYCA #1 (fingering) Rauma Finull PT2 (100% Norwegian wool, 191 yd/175 m / 50 g)
CYCA #1 (fingering) Rauma 2-ply Gammelserie (100% Norwegian wool, 175 yd/160 m / 50 g)

Yarn Colors and Amounts:
Finull PT2: Pink 479: 50 (50) g
Gammelserie: Sheep's Black 410: 50 (50) g

Needles:
U. S. size 1.5 / 2.5 mm: set of 5 dpn

GAUGE
28 sts = 4 in / 10 cm.
Adjust needle size to obtain correct gauge if necessary.
The women's size is small and close-fitting. If you want slightly larger mittens, you can use needles U. S. 2.5 /3 mm and work to a gauge of 26 sts in 4 in / 10 cm.

RIGHT MITTEN
With Black, CO 72 (72) sts. Divide sts evenly onto 4 dpn and join; pm for beginning of rnd. Begin with a two-end braid as explained on page 15. Next, work pattern on Chart 1. On the last rnd of women's size, decrease evenly spaced around to 60 sts. Make another two-end braid.

Now work following Chart 2. Where indicated on chart, set aside 11 (13) sts for thumb on scrap yarn (see page 14). Continue in pattern until mitten reaches nail of little finger.

Shape top as shown on Chart 3. You will decrease every 6th st a total of 4 times. Continue with Pink only, working (k2tog) around, knit 1 rnd, (k2tog) around. Cut yarn and draw end through rem sts; tighten.

THUMB
Pick up and knit 13 + 13 (15 + 15) sts—total of 26 (30) sts around thumbhole (see page 14).
Women's size: *At the same time* as beginning charted pattern, k11, k2tog, k11, k2tog = 24 sts rem for thumb.
Men's size: Knit around without decreasing = 30 sts total.
Make sure thumb pattern aligns with pattern on hand.
Work around in stockinette pattern following Chart 4 for women (men) 2 (3) times. Knit 1 rnd Pink without decreasing, then k2tog around. Cut yarn and draw end through rem sts; tighten.

LEFT MITTEN
Work as for right mitten, reversing chart so thumb is on left side of palm.

FINISHING
Weave in all ends neatly on WS. Wash mittens gently in lukewarm water and wool-safe soap. Dry flat until completely dry.

Hat with Snowflakes

Stars and snowflakes of all sorts have been a common motif on knitted Norwegian textiles. They are featured on both traditional textiles and garments by contemporary Norwegian designers. I chose blue and white for my snowflake hat.

The stocking cap was originally a men's hat. We've found the first traces of these caps in Phrygia, now in Turkey, in antique times. In the Roman Empire, we know that slaves were presented with a red cap when they were freed. During the French Revolution, red caps were very popular. Here in Norway, the earliest evidence of a stocking cap comes from a glass painting from 1700, but they were probably popular for a good while before then. Red stocking caps were seen in all areas of Norway, in the interior and along the coasts from south to north. Blue stocking caps were also common in many places.

Fishermen's hats had to fit well around their foreheads, and they often wore stocking caps that were then covered with a leather or wool hat. Even when southwesters (waterproof hats) became common, many continued to wear knitted stocking caps underneath. These caps might or might not have had a pompom on top, and pompoms took various forms. Some caps were single-color, while others were patterned.

Some of these stocking caps were imported, but most were knitted by wives or sweethearts. This hat has much in common with stocking caps from Telemark.

INSTRUCTIONS

Skill Level: Intermediate

SIZES
Women's (Men's)

FINISHED MEASUREMENTS
Circumference: 19¾ (23¾) in / 50 (60) cm

MATERIALS
Yarn:
CYCA #1 (fingering) Isager Strik Tweed (70% wool, 30% mohair, 219 yd/200m / 50 g)

Yarn Colors and Amounts:
Blue Denim: 50 (50) g
Raw White: 50 (50) g

Needles:
U. S. size 0 / 2 mm: short circular and set of 5 dpn

GAUGE
36 sts x 31 rnds = 4 x 4 in / 10 x 10 cm. Adjust needle size to obtain correct gauge if necessary.

HAT
With Blue and short circular, CO 180 (216) sts. Join, being careful not to twist cast-on row; pm for beginning of rnd. Work around in k2, p2 ribbing for ⅜ in / 1 cm. Now work in pattern following chart. When hat measures 4¾ (6) in / 12 (15) cm, begin shaping top if you want a short hat. If you prefer a baggy hat, knit 2-4 in / 5-10 cm more before decreasing. Change to dpn when sts no longer fit around circular.

Top Shaping
Decrease Rnd 1: *K7, k2tog*; rep * to * around. Knit 9 rnds.
Decrease Rnd 2: *K6, k2tog*; rep * to * around. Knit 8 rnds.
Decrease Rnd 3: *K5, k2tog*; rep * to * around. Knit 7 rnds.
Decrease Rnd 4: *K4, k2tog*; rep * to * around. Knit 6 rnds.
Decrease Rnd 5: *K3, k2tog*; rep * to * around. Knit 5 rnds.
Decrease Rnd 6: *K2, k2tog*; rep * to * around. Knit 4 rnds.
Decrease Rnd 7: *K1, k2tog*; rep * to * around. Knit 3 rnds.
Decrease Rnd 8: *K2tog*; rep * to * around. Knit 2 rnds.
Decrease Rnd 9: *K2tog*; rep * to * around. Cut yarn and draw end through rem sts; tighten.

FINISHING
Weave in all ends neatly on WS. Gently steam press hat under a damp pressing cloth to block. Make a pompom with White and Blue yarn, about 2-2¾ in / 5-7 cm in diameter. Sew pompom securely to top of hat.

Embroidered Setesdal Sweater for Men

The first traces of traditional Setesdal sweaters with lice and X-O patterns date to around 1850. The cross and circle motif was a religious symbol, used in tapestries and coverlets and on bands and head coverings in several places in Norway, but it was especially common in Setesdal. The cross is a local representation of an Andrew cross with diagonal arms, formed as for the letter X. A circle (*kringle*) depicts arms crossed over the chest, a common method of praying in the Middle Ages.

A pencil drawing of twenty-two-year-old Arne Bjugsen Sagneskar, made in 1848 by Adolph Tidemand, depicts what seems to be a knitted pullover. In a photograph of a man named Grunde Grundesson Austad from the late 1850s, we can clearly see a knitted lice sweater (*lusekofte*). We can also discern cuffs with lovely embroidery, and buttons on the lower edges of the sleeves.

In Vestland, the edge of the neck and sometimes also the sleeves might be decorated with colorful rose bands or handwoven bands. In Setesdal, they were always edged with *vadmal* or *klede* (two types of fulled woven fabric), embellished with embroidery.

The oldest sweaters had only one zigzag panel over the shoulders and at the top of the sleeves. The limited amount of embellishment is connected to a religious revival in the villages in Setesdal between 1830 and 1860, when Haugeanism (a movement dedicated to, among other things, frugality, and by extension minimal decoration) gained a strong foothold.

Later, the number of panels increased. A definitive text from the time period discussing how the panels should be knitted, or in what sequence, hasn't been found.

Halvard M. Holen (born in 1880) before he boarded a ship bound for America in 1900 and settled in Minnesota.

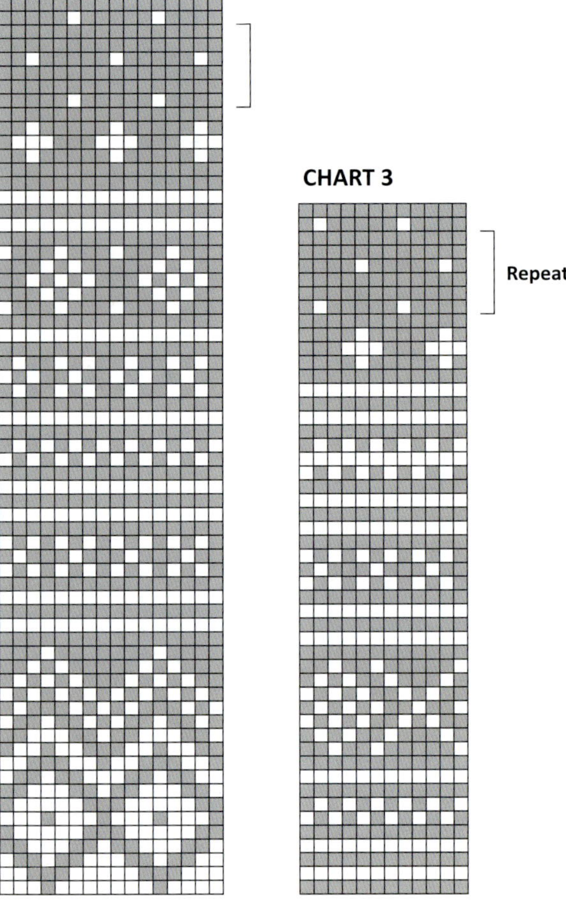
CHART 1
CHART 3
Repeat

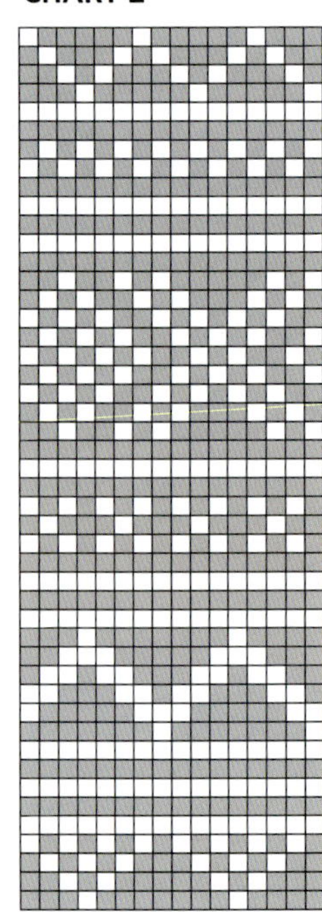
CHART 2

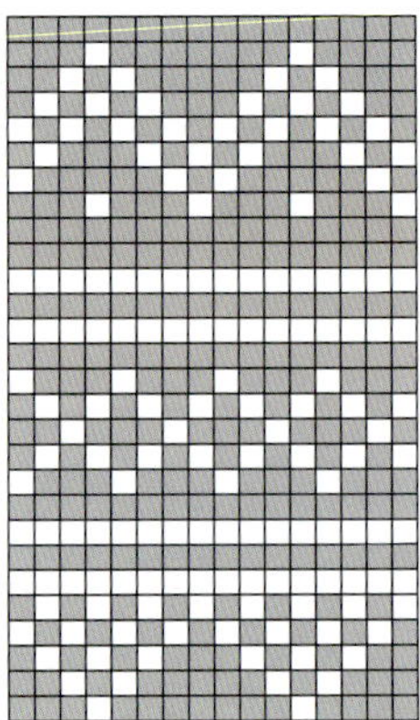
CHART 4

Natural White
Sheep's Black

INSTRUCTIONS

Skill Level: Experienced

SIZES
S (M, L, XL, XXL)

FINISHED MEASUREMENTS
Chest: 39¾ (42¼, 45¼, 48¾, 52½) in / 101 (107, 115, 124, 133) cm
Sleeve Length: 19¾ (20, 20½, 21, 21) in / 50 (51, 52, 53, 53) cm
Total Length: 28 (28¼, 28¾, 29¼, 29½) in / 71 (72, 73, 74, 75) cm

MATERIALS
Yarn:
CYCA #1 (fingering) Rauma 2-ply Gammelserie (100% Norwegian wool, 175 yd/160 m / 50 g)

Yarn Colors and Amounts:
Natural White 401: 150 (150, 150, 200, 200) g
Sheep's Black 410: 350 (350, 350, 400, 400) g

Needles:
U. S. sizes 0 and 1.5 / 2 and 2.5 mm: circular and set of 5 dpn

GAUGE
27 sts x 34 rnds = 4 x 4 in / 10 x 10 cm.
Adjust needle size to obtain correct gauge if necessary.

BODY
With Natural White and smaller circular, CO 272 (288, 312, 336, 360) sts. Join, being careful not to twist cast-on row; pm for beginning of rnd. Work around in k2, p2 ribbing for 2 in / 5 cm. Work in stockinette until body measures 4¾ (4¾, 4¾, 4¾, 4¾) in / 12 (12, 12, 12, 12) cm. Change to larger circular (check gauge for stranded colorwork and adjust needle size to maintain correct gauge). Work in pattern following Chart 1. Continue lice pattern until body measures 21¾ (22, 22, 22¾, 23¼) in / 55 (56, 57, 58, 59) cm. Work pattern following Chart 2. Turn work inside so front RS faces back RS. Hold the needles parallel. With a third needle, work 3-needle bind-off: K2tog with first st of each needle. *K2tog with next

pair of sts; pass 1st st on right needle over 2nd. Continue from * until all sts have been bound off. As you work across, make sure patterns align. When 1 loop rem, cut yarn and draw end through loop.

SLEEVES
With Black and smaller dpn, CO 64 (68, 72, 76, 80) sts. Divide sts onto 4 dpn and join, being careful not to twist cast-on row; pm for beginning of rnd. Work around in k2, p2 ribbing for ⅜ in / 1 cm. Work in stockinette until body measures 5¼ in / 13 cm. Now work in pattern following Chart 3 and then lice. *At the same time*, every 6th rnd, increase 2 sts centered on underarm until there are a total of 100 (106, 112, 118, 124) sts. Continue in lice pattern until sleeve measures 16¼ (16½, 17, 17¼, 17¼) in / 41 (42, 43, 44, 44) cm and then work panels of Chart 4. Turn sleeve inside out and, with Black, knit around for 1¼ in / 3 cm for facing. BO loosely. Make second sleeve the same way.

FINISHING
Weave in all ends neatly on WS. Measure sleeve top across width and measure down side of body for sleeve depth. Reinforce armhole by crocheting or machine-stitching 2 lines on each side of center st. Carefully cut armhole open up center st on each side. Attach sleeves with mattress stitch. Fold sleeve facing to WS and sew down to cover cut edges. Gently steam press sweater under a damp pressing cloth.

EMBROIDERY
You can order embroidery kits for the neck (an "antique neck"—*antikk hals*) and sleeve cuffs by emailing Setesdal Husflid (post@setesdal-husflid.no). The kit instructions suggest how to work the embroidery.

Setesdal Sweater for Women

Jorunn Jondsdotter Rysstad (born in 1909, married name Fjermestad) believed she was perhaps the first woman to wear a lice sweater in Setesal. There are two photos of her from about 1930, wearing a pullover with lice and traditional Setesdal panels. They were taken by the traveling photographer Gunnar Å. Helle. "I took the patterns at random," she is reported to have said. She also said that many were alarmed by her. The fact that she wore traditional men's clothing was absolutely sensational at the time.

Jorunn Jondsdotter Rysstad in a sweater she designed in about 1930.

Some years later, in 1942, Gyro Rynestad began knitting the same patterns for women and men.

"Some travelling people showed their old [traditional] sweaters that were admired for the pretty patterns on them."

Rynestad knitted more than 100 sweaters and sold them; the first was for a grocer's wife in Kristiansand.

In the modern day, it isn't unusual for women and men to wear the same knitted sweaters, and it's easy to forget that patterned sweaters—whether from Setesdal, Fana, or Nordfjord—were originally men's garments.

CHART 2

CHART 4

CHART 1

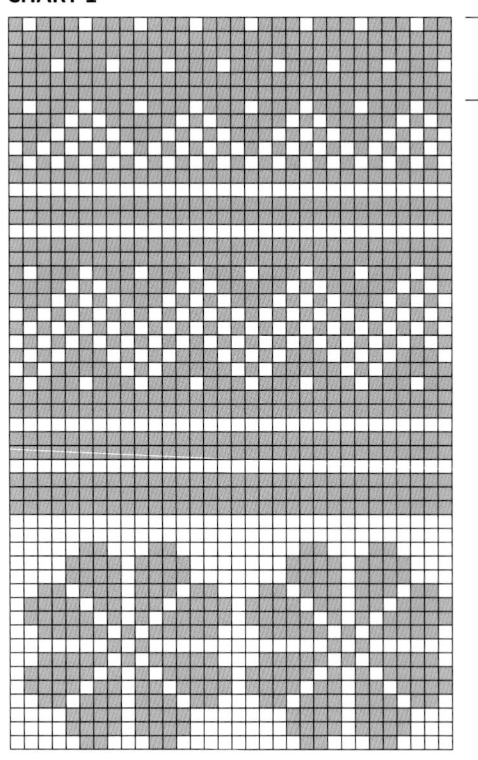

CHART 3

INSTRUCTIONS

Skill Level: Experienced

SIZES
S (M, L, XL, XXL)

FINISHED MEASUREMENTS
Chest: 38¼ (40¼, 42½, 45, 47¼) in / 97 (102, 108, 114, 120) cm
Sleeve Length: 18¼ (18½, 19, 19¼, 19¾) in / 46 (47, 48, 49, 50) cm
Total Length: 23¾ (24, 24½, 24¾, 25¼) in / 60 (61, 62, 63, 64) cm

MATERIALS
Yarn:
CYCA #1 (fingering) Rauma 2-ply Gammelserie (100% Norwegian wool, 175 yd/160 m / 50 g)

Yarn Colors and Amounts:
Natural White 401: 100 (150, 150, 200, 200) g
Sheep's Black 410: 350 (350, 350, 400, 400) g

Needles:
U. S. sizes 0 and 1.5 / 2 and 2.5 mm: circular and set of 5 dpn

GAUGE
28 sts x 35 rnds = 4 x 4 in / 10 x 10 cm.
Adjust needle size to obtain correct gauge if necessary.

BODY
With Natural White and smaller circular, CO 272 (288, 304, 320, 336) sts. Join, being careful not to twist cast-on row; pm for beginning of rnd. Work around in k2, p2 ribbing for 2 in / 5 cm. Work in stockinette until body measures 4 (4, 4, 4, 4) in / 10 (10, 10, 10, 10) cm. Change to larger circular (check gauge for stranded colorwork and adjust needle size to maintain correct gauge). Work in pattern following Chart 1. Continue lice pattern until body measures 18½ (19, 19¼, 19¾, 20) in / 47 (48, 49, 50, 51) cm. Work pattern following Chart 2. Turn work inside so front RS faces back RS. Hold the needles parallel. With a third needle, work 3-needle bind-off: K2tog with first st of each needle. *K2tog with next pair of sts; pass 1st st on right needle over 2nd. Continue from * until all sts have been bound off. As you work across, make sure patterns align. When 1 loop rem, cut yarn and draw end through loop.

SLEEVES
With Black and larger dpn, CO 52 (56, 60, 64, 68) sts. Divide sts onto 4 dpn and join, being careful not to twist cast-on row; pm for beginning of rnd. Work around in k2, p2 ribbing for 2½ in / 6 cm. Now work in pattern following Chart 3 and then lice. *At the same time*, every 6th rnd, increase 2 sts centered on underarm until there are a total of 94 (100, 106, 112, 118) sts. Continue in lice pattern until sleeve measures 12¾ (13, 13½, 13¾, 14¼) in / 32 (33, 34, 35, 36) cm and then work panels of Chart 4. Turn sleeve inside out and, with Black, knit around for 1¼ in / 3 cm for facing. BO loosely. Make second sleeve the same way.

FINISHING
Weave in all ends neatly on WS. Mark the width of neck opening. Reinforce opening by crocheting or machine-stitching 2 lines on each side of bind-off row. Cut open carefully. With Black, using a crochet hook if desired to lift sts onto needle, pick up and knit 3 sts for every 4 sts—except at center front and center back, where you will pick up in every st. With smaller circular, purl 1 rnd, knit 6 rnds, purl 1 rnd, knit 6 rnds and BO. Fold neckband at purl rnd and sew edge down on WS to cover cut edges.

Measure sleeve top across width and measure down side of body for sleeve depth. Reinforce armhole opening by crocheting or machine-stitching 2 lines on each side of center st. Carefully cut armhole open up center st on each side. Attach sleeves with mattress stitch. Fold sleeve facing to WS and sew down to cover cut edges.

   Gently steam press sweater under a damp pressing cloth.

Hat with Setesdal Motifs

INSTRUCTIONS

Skill Level: Intermediate-Experienced

SIZES
Women's (Men's)

FINISHED MEASUREMENTS
Circumference: 21 (23¾) in / 53 (60) cm

MATERIALS
Yarn:
CYCA #2 (fingering) Rauma Tumi (50% alpaca, 50% wool, 142 yd/130 m / 50 g)

Yarn Colors and Amounts:
White SFN10: 50 (50) g
Black SFN50: 50 (50) g

Needles:
U. S. size 2.5 / 3 mm: short circular and set of 5 dpn

GAUGE
27 sts x 31 rnds = 4 x 4 in / 10 x 10 cm. Adjust needle size to obtain correct gauge if necessary.

HAT
With circular and White, CO 144 (160) sts. Join, being careful not to twist cast-on row; pm for beginning of rnd. Work around in k2, p2 ribbing for 1¼ (2½) in / 3 (6) cm. Now work in stockinette pattern following chart. When hat is 7 (8) in / 18 (20) cm long, pm at every 36th (32nd) st. Decrease on each side of each marker with k2tog before marker and ssk after marker. Knit 3 rnds. Change to dpn when sts no longer fit around circular. Now decrease on every other rnd 5 times. Decrease on every rnd until it is no longer possible to work lice. Cut yarn and draw end through rem sts; tighten.

FINISHING
Weave in all ends neatly on WS. Gently steam press hat under a damp pressing cloth to block. Make a pompom with White and Black yarn, about 2¾ in / 7 cm in diameter. Sew pompom securely to top of hat.

☐ White
▨ Black

CHART

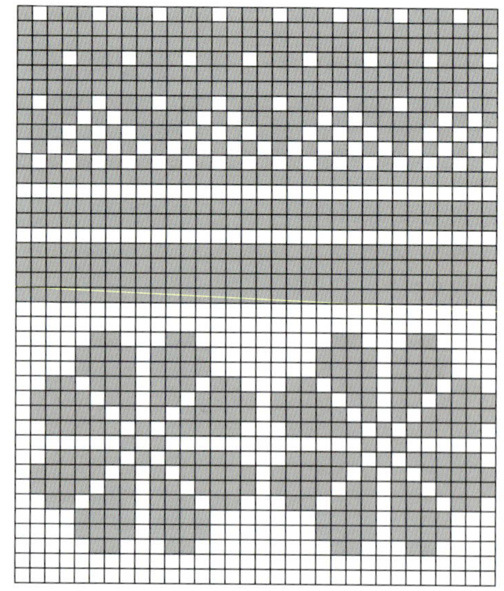

"

Jon Nomeland's Pullover

Interest in photography, and the search for photographers to take people's pictures, exploded when mass development of photographs became technically possible in the 1860s. "Visiting card fever" spread throughout Norway—everyone wanted to have photos of themselves to make visiting cards, which could be given out to family and friends.

Knud Knudsen (1832-1915) established himself as a photographer with his own studio in Bergen in 1864. He also took his cameras, glass plates, chemicals, and dark room tent on numerous trips all around the county. His photos were titled and numbered for listings in his sale catalogue, which means it's possible to follow Knudsen's travels around Norway. Since the glass plates used have the photo date engraved, many of his photos can be dated precisely.

Knudsen's first trip to Setesdal was in 1875. He photographed, among others, Jon O. Nomeland and his family, from Hylestad. Nomeland and his wife sat on a bench in front, with their younger children in their laps or next to them. Their older children stood in back. Everyone looks serious; in those days, photos needed long exposures, sometimes several minutes, and it was difficult to hold any other facial expression long enough to be sure the picture wouldn't be blurred.

Nomeland is wearing a knitted lice sweater. It doesn't have many panels at the lower edge, nor at the tops of the sleeves or shoulders; typically, the oldest lice sweaters were made this way. This sweater also doesn't have felt fabric with embroidery on the sleeve cuffs. The bottom few centimeters has a rather simple pattern, which makes a nice edge. Most of the sweater is hidden behind the bib on his pants and the little vest he has on over it. It's very likely that the lower part of the sweater was natural sheep's white, and possibly there was a narrow panel before the lice section.

I decided to use a heavier and softer yarn than the original, and I copied the pattern on the sleeves and top panel on the shoulders. At the lower part of the body, I repeated the fine sleeve panel we can see. The sweater has ties on the bottom edge and a removeable neckband/cowl that can also be tied.

Jon O. Nomeland with his family, Hylestad in Setesdal, 1875.

Natural Gray
Natural Sheep's White

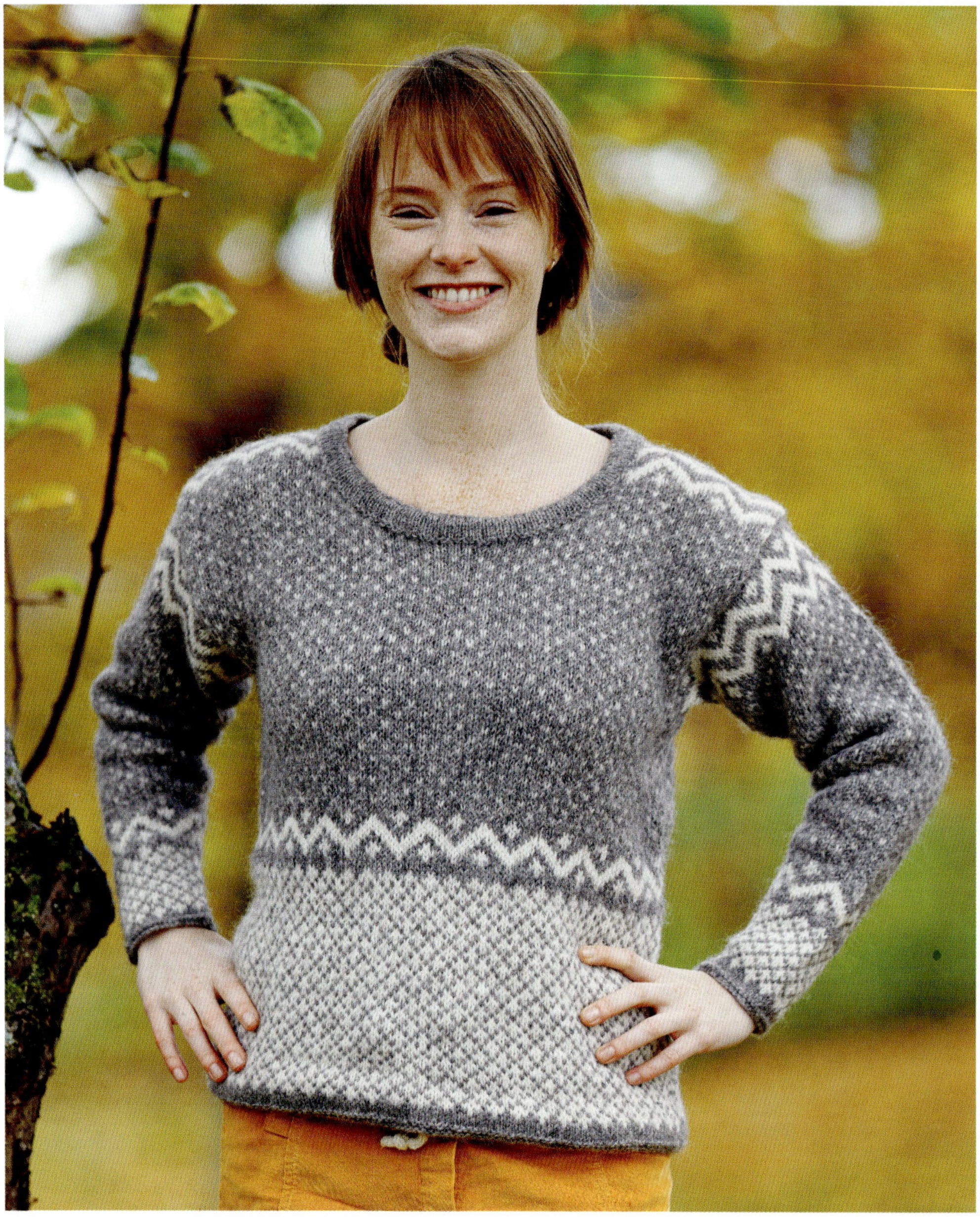

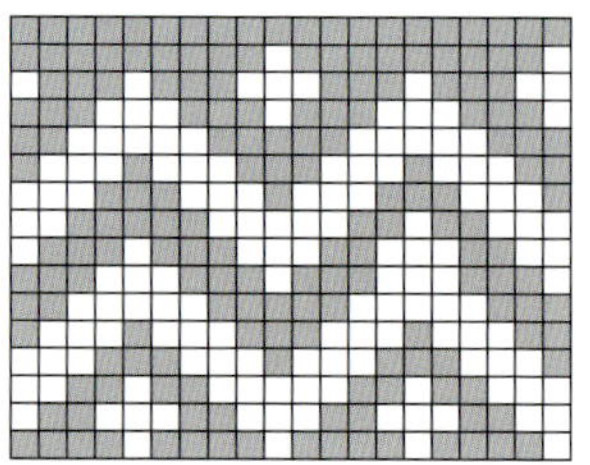

CHART 3

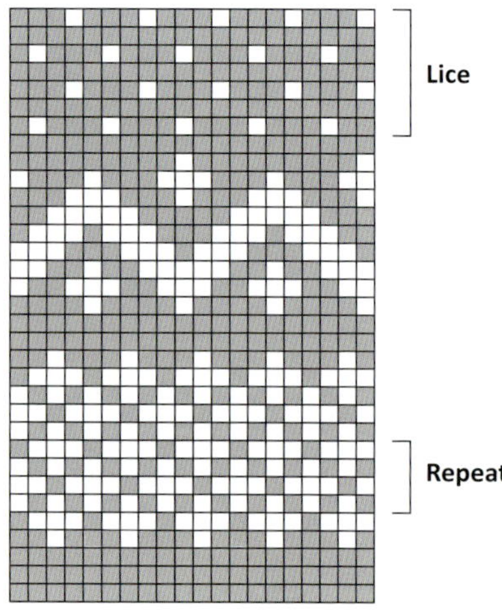

CHART 2

CHART 1

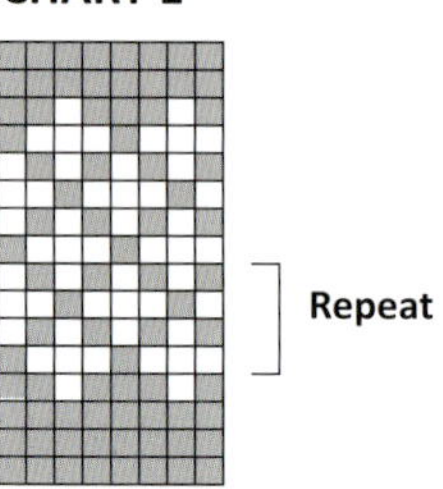

INSTRUCTIONS

Skill Level: Experienced

SIZES
S (M, L, XL, XXL)

FINISHED MEASUREMENTS
Chest: 36 (39½, 43, 46½, 50) in / 91 (100, 109, 118, 127) cm
Sleeve Length: 18¼ (18½, 19, 19¼, 19¾) in / 46 (47, 48, 49, 50) cm
Total Length: 23¾ (24, 24½, 24¾, 25¼) in / 60 (61, 62, 63, 64) cm

MATERIALS
Yarn:
CYCA #3 (DK, light worsted) Hillesvåg Tinde pelsullgarn (100% Norwegian wool, 284 yd/260 m / 100 g)
CYCA #2 (sport, baby) Hillesvåg Sol lamullgarn (100% Norwegian lamb's wool, 317 yd/290 m / 50 g)

Yarn Colors and Amounts:
Tinde Natural Gray 652115: 250 (250, 300, 300, 350) g
Sol Natural White 58400: 200 (200, 250, 250, 300) g

Needles:
U. S. sizes 6 and 0 / 4 and 2 mm (smaller size is for neckband): circular and set of 5 dpn

GAUGE
22 sts x 24 rnds = 4 x 4 in / 10 x 10 cm. Adjust needle size to obtain correct gauge if necessary.

BODY
With Gray and larger circular, CO 200 (220, 240, 260, 280) sts. Begin with facing on lower edge. Work back and forth in stockinette for 1½ in / 4 cm. Join and purl 1 rnd, knit 1 rnd, purl 1 rnd. The opening on the facing is at center front. Cut yarn and begin at the side so you have 100 (110, 120, 130, 140) sts each for back and front. There should be 50 (55, 60, 65, 70) sts from the side marker to the split. Continue in stockinette pattern following Chart 1 until body measures 8 in / 20 cm above facing. Now work following Chart 2, repeating lice above panel until body measures 21¼ (21¾, 22, 22½, 22¾) in / 54 (55, 56, 57, 58) cm from the lowest garter ridge. Work following Chart 3.

Turn work inside out so front RS faces back RS. Hold the needles parallel. With a third needle, work 3-needle bind-off: K2tog with first st of each needle. *K2tog with next pair of sts; pass 1st st on right needle over 2nd. Continue from * until all sts have been bound off. As you work across, make sure patterns align. When 1 loop rem, cut yarn and draw end through loop.

SLEEVES
With Gray and larger dpn, CO 44 (48, 52, 56, 60) sts. Divide sts onto 4 dpn and join, being careful not to twist cast-on row; pm for beginning of rnd. Knit 1 rnd, purl 1 rnd, knit 1 rnd, purl 1 rnd. Now work in pattern following Chart 2 until lower section measures 3¼ in /

8 cm before you end with the zigzag panel. Continue in lice pattern and, *at the same time*, every 5th rnd, increase 2 sts centered on underarm until there are a total of 90 (94, 98, 102, 106) sts. Continue in lice pattern until sleeve measures 17 (17¼, 17¾, 18¼, 18½) in / 43 (44, 45, 46, 47) cm, and then work Chart 3. Turn sleeve inside out; with Gray, knit around for 1¼ in / 3 cm for facing. BO loosely. Make second sleeve the same way.

REMOVEABLE NECKBAND/COWL
With Gray and larger circular, CO 140 sts. Join, being careful not to twist cast-on row; pm for beginning of rnd. Work around in stockinette for ¾ in / 2 cm. Purl 1 rnd, knit 1 rnd, purl 1 rnd, and then work following Chart 1 until piece measures 6¼ in / 16 cm. Now work back and forth in stockinette for 3 rows with Gray. Purl 1 rnd, knit 1 rnd, purl 1 rnd, then knit around for ¾ in / 2 cm. BO.

I-CORDS
With large dpn, CO 4 sts and knit an I-cord (as described on page 12) until it is 47¼ (51¼, 55¼, 59, 63) in / 120 (130, 140, 150, 160) cm long. Make another cord 35½ in / 90 cm long.

FINISHING
Weave in all ends neatly on WS. Fold facing at lower edge of body to WS and sew down. Mark width of neck opening. Reinforce opening by crocheting or machine-stitching 2 lines on each side of bind-off row. Cut open carefully. With Gray, using a crochet hook to lift sts onto needle, pick up and knit 3 sts for every 4 sts—except at center front and center back, where you will pick up in every st. With smaller circular, purl 1 rnd. Knit 6 rnds, purl 1 rnd, knit 6 rnds and BO. Fold neckband at purl rnd and sew edge down on WS to cover cut edges.

Measure sleeve top across width and measure down side of body for sleeve depth. Reinforce armhole opening by crocheting or machine-stitching 2 lines on each side of center st. Carefully cut armhole open up center st on each side. Attach sleeves with mattress stitch. Fold sleeve facing to WS and sew down to cover cut edges.

Fold facing at lower edge of body to WS and sew down. Thread the long cord through casing on body and the short cord through casing on cowl. Knot each end of each cord. Gently steam press sweater under a damp pressing cloth.

Ullbol Pullover
from Rogaland

In 1934, a woman from Vigrestad on Jæren was indicted for selling knitted garments in the town square in Stavanger. According to a commercial law from 1933,
no one was allowed to sell "finished clothing" by peddling or in the square. At
the trial, she testified that she had had a stall on the town square since early in
the 1920s, and that the police had agreed that she didn't need a commercial or
business letter to sell there. She refused, therefore, to pay a fine of 5 crowns or,
alternatively, to spend one day in jail.

Several woman explained to the judge that they also sold sweaters in the square.
One woman from Brusand confirmed that she had conducted her business there,
selling knitted sweaters and undergarments, for more than forty years.

The judge decided it wasn't appropriate to refuse these women the right to sell
knitted goods; he ruled that "finished clothing" meant "finished sewn clothing,"
ready-to-wear and commercially-made, and therefore the 1933 law didn't apply to
knitted goods or handmade sweaters. Therefore, the woman from Vigrestad could
go free and could continue selling her wares in the town square.

Among the most popular garments sold in the square in Stavanger was the *ullbolen*,
or "wool bodice," a ribbed undergarment. It was especially popular among young
people in the 1960s and 1970s. International tourists were delighted by under-
dresses, which could technically be worn on their own. The women of Stavanger
shook their heads at these foreigners who wanted to go about in only undercloth-
ing, but were perfectly happy to sell those under-
clothes to them.

Inspired by the wool bodices of Rogaland, I
designed a ribbed sweater with raglan shaping.
My sweater pattern has vertical stripes, as did
the original garments, but unlike their forebears,
these sweaters are knitted in two colors.

*Knitted under-sweater from Visnes on Karmøy,
made sometime between 1945 and 1989.*

INSTRUCTIONS

Skill Level: Experienced

SIZES
S (M, L, XL, XXL)

FINISHED MEASUREMENTS
Hip: 37¾ (40¼, 42½, 45¾, 48) in / 96 (102, 108, 116, 122) cm

Chest: 36¾ (39, 41¼, 43¾, 46) in / 93 (99, 105, 111, 117) cm
Waist: 36¾ (39, 41¼, 43¾, 46) in / 93 (99, 105, 111, 117) cm
Sleeve Length: 18¼ (18¼, 18½, 19, 19¼) in / 46 (46, 47, 48, 49) cm
Total Length: 26¾ (27½, 28¼, 29¼, 30) in / 68 (70, 72, 74, 76) cm

MATERIALS
Yarn:
Blue-White version: CYCA #1 (fingering) Rauma 2-ply Gammelserie (100% Norwegian wool, 175 yd/160 m / 50 g)
Red-Pink version: Gammmelserie and CYCA #1 (fingering) Rauma Finull PT2 (100% Norwegian wool, 191 yd/175 m / 50 g)

Yarn Colors and Amounts:
Blue-White version:
Natural White 401: 150 (200, 200, 250, 250) g
Blue 447: 200 (250, 250, 300, 300) g
Red-Pink version:
Gammelserie Red 424
Finull PT2: Pink 0456

Needles:
U. S. sizes 4 / 3.5 mm: circular and set of 5 dpn

GAUGE
25 sts x 27 rnds = 4 x 4 in / 10 x 10 cm.
Adjust needle size to obtain correct gauge if necessary.

BODY
With Blue and circular, CO 240 (256, 272, 288, 304) sts. Join, being careful not to twist cast-on row. Pm for beginning of rnd and at side = 120 (128, 136, 144, 152) sts each for front and back.
Rnd 1: *K2 with Blue, k2 with White*; rep * to * around.
Rnd 2: *K2 with Blue, p2 with White*; rep * to * around.
Rep Rnd 2, working purl sts a little loosely for a relief st effect, until body measures 4¼ in / 11 cm. At each side, k2Blue tog.
Work 3 more rnds and then decrease 1 more Blue st at each side.
Continue, decreasing 1 st at each side on every 4th rnd a total of 4 times = 232 (248, 264, 280, 296) sts rem.
Continue without decreasing until body measures 15½ (15¾ 16¼, 16½, 17) in / 39 (40, 41, 42, 43) cm, and then BO 10 sts centered at each side for underarms.

SLEEVES
With Blue and dpn, CO 44 (48, 52, 58, 62) sts. Divide sts onto 4 dpn and join.
Rnd 1: *K2 with Blue, k2 with White*; rep * to * around.
Rnd 2: *K2 with Blue, p2 with White*; rep * to * around.
Rep Rnd 2, working purl sts a little loosely for a relief st effect, for 20 rnds.
Increase 2 sts with Blue centered on underarm. Increase the same way on every 4th rnd, with Blue or White to maintain stripe sequence. When increasing with White, knit the first and last sts. Increase as est until sleeve measures 18¼ (18¼, 18½, 19, 19¼) in / 46 (46, 47, 48, 49) cm and there are 96 (100, 104, 108, 112) sts total. BO 10 sts centered on underarm. Make the second sleeve the same way.

RAGLAN SHAPING
Arrange body and sleeves on circular for a total of 384 (408, 432, 456, 480) sts. Pm at each junction of body and sleeve. Begin at the back and one sleeve. Continue in vertical stripes with knit over knit in Blue and purl over purl in White. *At the same time,* decrease as follows:
Rnd 1: K2Blue tog, sl next Blue st knitwise, k1 Blue, psso. You now have 2 Blue sts at the junction. These 2 sts should be knit with Blue throughout.
***Rnd 2:** Work as est without decreasing.
Rnd 3: When you come to a junction, p2White tog, k2 Blue, p2White tog.
Rnd 4: Work as est without decreasing.
Rnd 5: When you come to a junction, k2tog with 1 Blue and 1 White, k2Blue tog, with Blue, k2tog tbl with 1 White and 1 Blue.
Rnd 6: Work as est without decreasing.
Rnd 7: When you come to a junction, k2Blue tog, k2 Blue, sl 1 Blue, k1 Blue, psso.*
Rep * to * until 42 (46, 50, 54, 58) sts rem on the front between the 2 Blue diagonal stripes.

Now decrease only on front and back, not the sleeves, 4 times = 120 (128, 136, 144, 152) sts total rem. Work in pattern for 1¼ in / 3 cm without decreasing.
Round the front neck by working up to the raglan decrease line on the front; turn and work to raglan decrease line on the other side of front. Turn and work to raglan line again but stop 2 sts before last turn. Turn. Work to raglan line again but stop 2 sts before last turn. Continue with short rows, the same way until back is ¾ in 2 cm higher then front. End with 1 rnd over all sts.
BO with Blue by working k2, sl 1st st over last, *k1, sl 1st st over last; rep from * all around. Make sure bind-off is not too tight. (If you want a slightly tighter neckline, before binding off, you can purl 1 rnd with Blue and then knit a facing for 1¼ in / 3 cm in the same color. Fold facing at purl rnd and sew down on WS.)

FINISHING
Seam underarms. Weave in all ends neatly on WS. Gently steam press on WS under a damp pressing cloth.

Shawl from Karmsund

At the Karmsund Folk Museum and Haugland Museum, you'll find a traditional triangular shawl knitted with gray wool. What's special about this shawl is the finishing, which has pretty triangular points. It was a little difficult to tell whether the points were crocheted or knitted, but I let myself be inspired to knit them. The neckline is edged with crocheted loops of "mouse teeth."

The shawl has ties at the long tips so it can be crossed over the chest and tied behind the back, as was common in the last half of the nineteenth century. This type of knitted shawl was a common everyday garment all around Norway; some are embellished with lace patterns, and others feature colorful stripes. In this case, the edging is the distinguishing feature, and this shawl is easy to knit and very warm.

INSTRUCTIONS

Skill Level: Advanced Beginner

FINISHED MEASUREMENTS
Length: 82 in / 208 cm
Width: at widest point, 30¾ in / 78 cm

MATERIALS
Yarn:
CYCA #2 (sport, baby) Lofoten Wool 2-ply Skarv
(100% Norwegian wool, 344 yd/315 m / 100 g)

Yarn Color and Amount:
Indigo Blue: 10 skeins

Needles:
U. S. size 7 / 4.5 mm: circular

Crochet Hook:
U. S. size G-6 / 4 mm

Notions:
43 stitch markers

GAUGE
17 sts x 18 ridges (= 36 rows) = 4 x 4 in /
10 x 10 cm.
Adjust needle size to obtain correct gauge if
necessary.

GARMENT CONSTRUCTION
The shawl is knitted in garter st (= knit all rows).
It begins at the top of center back, is worked
back and forth, and increased on each side and
at the center.

SHAWL
CO 3 sts. Knit 1 row.
Row 1: Kb&f (= knit into back loop as for k1tbl,
k1 into front loop as for regular knit, slip both
sts off left needle), yo, k1, yo, k1 = 6 sts total.
Row 2: Kb&f into 1st st, knit to end of row = 7
sts.
Row 3: Kb&f into 1st st, k2, yo, k1 (= center st,
pm around this st), yo, k3 = 10 sts total.

Row 4: Kb&f into 1st st, knit to end of row = 11
sts.
Continue as est with kb&f at beginning of
every row and yo on each side of center st
on odd-numbered rows (= 3 sts increased).
Even-numbered rows begin with kb&f and then
are knit to end of row—1 st increased. Rows
3-4 are the 1st and 2nd pattern rows = 1 garter
ridge.

Continue as est until shawl measures approx.
27½ in / 70 cm down the center and there are
352 sts total. Pm at center and every 16th st (=
21 markers total).
Continue as before, but, on the first pattern
row, increase 1 st on each side of each marker.
Rep 6 times.
Place new markers, centered between the
previous markers (= 22 additional markers).
Continue as before, but, at the new markers,
decrease on each side of each marker with
k2tog tbl before marker and k2tog after marker
on the first pattern row. Rep 2 times and
remove the additional markers.
Knit 2 ridges, increasing on each side of each of
the original 21 markers. BO.

Crocheted Edging: Crochet loops along the lon-
gest edge: *1 sc, ch 3, skip 1 ridge.* Rep * to *
across and end with 1 sc.

FINISHING
Weave in all ends neatly on WS. The shawl
should be stretched and pinned out so the
edges of the triangular points will be neat
and smooth. You can first wash the shawl in
wool-safe soap and lukewarm water. Rinse
in same-temperature water. Gently squeeze
out excess water and then roll in a terrycloth
towel to remove more water. Pin the shawl
to a blocking mat or Styrofoam board. Or you
can pin out the shawl first and spray it with
lukewarm water. Leave shawl pinned out until
completely dry, at least 24 hours.

Garter-Striped Fana Sweater for Women

One style of sweater that's considerably different from many traditional Norwegian patterned sweaters is the garter-stitch cardigan from Fana. White sweaters were Sunday dress and garments for special occasions for men in that district, from the middle of the nineteenth century up to the present day. These sweaters were worn with colorfully embroidered suspenders, with a finishing touch in the form of a fine pocketwatch on a chain. Cardigans were closed with as many as 14 silver or pewter buttons to keep the closure neat and smooth.

Usually the lower edges of these cardigans had a couple two-end braids followed by block patterns, a stockinette panel with purl stitch patterns—a crown panel— and then garter stitch. Typically these same patterns would be repeated on the sleeves, but there are a few examples of sweaters with diamond patterns in traveling stitches. That was considered especially fine, as were rose motifs on the shoulders. All the cardigans were faced with cotton fabric on the wrong side and edged with red and white woven ribbons on both the front and cuffs.

"Cyclist and farmer" was the title of a photo taken by the amateur photographer Lauritz Johan Bekker Larsen (1877-1964) sometime between 1890 and 1910. In the photo, we see a strong older man— the farmer—wearing dark vadmal trousers and a cardigan typical of his region, with closely-spaced buttons down to the trousers, plus wide flower-patterned suspenders. Under the cardigan, he's wearing a white shirt buttoned at the neck. The cyclist is wearing pants and a jacket, white shirt, and tie.

I was inspired to make a version of this cardigan for women. It features diamond patterns on both body and sleeves. The buttonholes are sewn with pink thread instead of red, and I used a pink velvet ribbon along the front edges instead of the traditional red and white.

INSTRUCTIONS

Skill Level: Experienced

SIZES
S (M, L, XL, XXL)

FINISHED MEASUREMENTS
Chest: when buttoned, 38½ (41, 43¼, 45¾, 48¾) in / 98 (104, 110, 116, 124) cm + 2 in / 5 cm overlap
Hip: 34¾ (36¼, 37¾, 39½, 41¾) in / 88 (92, 96, 100, 106) cm
Waist: 36¾ (39, 41¼, 43¾, 46) in / 93 (99, 105, 111, 117) cm
Sleeve Length: 17¼ (17¾, 18¼, 18¼, 18½) in / 44 (45, 46, 46, 47) cm
Total Length: 21¾ (22½, 23¾, 24, 24½) in / 55 (57, 60, 61, 62) cm

MATERIALS
Yarn:
CYCA #1 (fingering) Rauma 2-ply Gammelserie (100% Norwegian wool, 175 yd/160 m / 50 g)

Yarn Color and Amounts:
Natural White 401: 400 (400, 450, 500, 550) g

Needles:
U. S. sizes 1.5 / 2.5 mm: circular and set of 5 dpn; cable needle

Notions:
Pink wool thread for buttonholes
Pink velvet ribbon, approx. 55 in / 140 cm
Pink twill tape for attaching buttons, approx. 21¾ in / 55 cm
Cotton canvas fabric for facings (single-color, floral, gingham, or striped)
10 (10, 11, 11, 11) silver or pewter buttons

GAUGE
25 sts x 52 rows (= 26 ridges) = 4 x 4 in / 10 x 10 cm.
Adjust needle size to obtain correct gauge if necessary.

BODY
With circular, CO 264 (276, 288, 300, 318) sts + 4 extra sts for steek (steek sts are not included in stitch counts; see page 8). Join, being careful not to twist cast-on row; pm for beginning of rnd. Work diamond pattern with cabled stitches following Chart 1. See chart Symbols Key for working cables with or without a cable needle. Work the repeat 4 times.

At the same time, begin buttonholes on right front. Make first buttonhole when body measures ¾ (1½, ¾, 1¼, 1½) in / 2 (4, 2, 3, 4) cm. Each buttonhole is worked over 6 sts, 5 sts inside right front edge:
Work 7 sts, slip next-to-last st over last st, *work 1 st, slip next-to-last st over last st; rep from * until you've bound off 6 sts. On the next rnd, CO 6 new sts over gap.
Make a buttonhole every 1½ in / 4 cm. There should be a total of 10 (10, 11, 11, 11) buttonholes on right front.

After completing Chart 1 pattern, knit 1 rnd, adjusting stitch count to 256 (272, 288, 304, 320) sts + steek. Purl 1 rnd, knit 1 rnd, purl 1 rnd = 2 ridges. Now work crown panel following chart 2. On the last rnd, adjust stitch count to 257 (273, 289, 305, 321) sts + steek.

After the crown pattern, BO steek sts and begin working back and forth in garter st.

As you continue, make the buttonholes as follows: When 11 sts rem on row, k2, slip 1st over 2nd, k1, slip 1st over 2nd, etc. until you've bound off 6 sts. Work last 4 sts on row. On next row, CO 6 sts over gap.

When body measures 13¾ (14, 15½ 15¾, 16¼) in / 35 (37, 39, 40, 41) cm, shape underarms as follows: K63 (67, 71, 75, 79), BO 10 sts, k111 (119, 127, 135, 143), BO 10 sts, k63 (67, 71, 75, 79). Now work each front and the back separately.

RIGHT FRONT
Continue in garter st and, *at the same time*, at armhole edge, BO 3 sts, then 2,2,1,1,1,1 1 sts = 51 (55, 59, 63, 67) sts rem.
When piece measures 17¾ (18½, 19¾, 20, 20½) in / 45 (47, 50, 51, 52) cm, BO 13 sts at front edge for neck, leaving room for last buttonhole = 38 (42, 46, 50, 54) sts rem. Round neckline: at neck edge, BO 3, then 2,2,1,1,1,1,1 sts = 26 (30, 34, 38, 42) sts rem.
Continue without further decreasing until piece measures 21¾ (22½, 23¾, 24, 24½) in / 55 (57, 60, 61, 62) cm. Place rem sts on a holder.

LEFT FRONT
Work as for right front, omitting buttonholes and reversing shaping to match.

BACK

Continue in garter st and, *at the same time*, at each armhole edge, BO 3 sts, then 2,2,1,1,1,1 sts = 87 (95, 103, 111, 119) sts rem. When back is 8 ridges shorter than front, at center, BO 15 sts for back neck. Work the two shoulders separately. BO 3, then 2,2,1,1,1 sts at side of neck = 26 (30, 34, 38, 42) sts rem for each shoulder.

SLEEVES

With dpn, CO 54 (60, 66, 72, 78) sts. Divide sts onto 4 dpn and join; pm for beginning of rnd. Work diamond pattern with cabled stitches following Chart 1 as for body. Knit 1 rnd, purl 1 rnd, knit 1 rnd, purl 1 rnd = 2 ridges. Now work crown panel following Chart 3.

Work the rest of the sleeve back and forth in garter st. *At the same time*, M1 after 1st st and M1 before last st of row every 5th ridge until sleeve measures 17¼ (17¾, 18¼, 18¼, 18½) in / 44 (45, 46, 46, 47) cm and there are 92 (98, 104, 110, 116) sts total.

Shape Armhole: At each side, BO 5 sts and then 3,2,2, sts and then BO 1 st 16 (17, 18, 19, 20) times. Finish sleeve cap: BO 2,2,2,3,3 sts and then 3 (5,5,5,5) sts, and finally 6 (6, 10, 14, 18) sts.

FINISHING

Weave in all ends neatly on WS. Machine- or hand-stitch 2 lines on each side of center steek st. Trim any excess fabric so you have a smooth, even edge from the neck down. Join shoulders with 3-needle bind-off: Slip held sts for one shoulder to dpn, with each set on a separate dpn. Hold the needles parallel, with RS facing RS. Using a third needle, k2tog with 1 st each from front and back. *K2tog with next pair of sts and slip 1st worked st on right needle over second. Rep from * until you've bound off all sts. Join 2nd shoulder the same way. Attach sleeves with mattress st and RS facing.

The sweater has a lining and trim of cotton canvas on the front and around the neck (see illustration on page 13). Wash the fabric first so that it shrinks before use. Add a seam allowance of approx. ⅜ in / 1 cm on each side in addition to the given measurements.

Begin with a strip 1½-2 in / 4-5 cm wide on each side of the neck, fold under and pin in place. Sew on down the long side from the neck shaping. Make another strip about 2¾ in / 7 cm wide around the neck and long enough out to the sides so it covers the ribbon you sewed on. Fold under and pin in place. Sew on down the long side which is not rounded. Fold at the corners and sew to the facing on the sides. Do the same on opposite front. Shape so the fabric follows the neckline shaping, fold in and pin in place. Trim to about 2-2½ in / 5-6 cm wide for the bands, pin in place and sew down from the opening. The facing is sewn by hand with whip st. The pink velvet ribbon is attached along the front edge and sewn to the facing all the way around.

With pink thread and buttonhole stitch, sew all around each buttonhole, through the facing. Cut through the facing to fit holes to buttons.

Use a twill tape sewn to facing to attach buttons (see page 13).

☐ **Knit**
ⓥ **Purl**

Crossing cables with cable needle:
Slip 1 st to cable needle and hold in front of work, k1, k1 from cable needle
Slip 1 st to cable needle and hold in back of work, k1, k1 from cable needle

Crossing cables without a cable needle:
K1tbl into 2nd st from behind work, knit 1st st and slip both sts from needle (it is easier to knit one st through back loop and it won't be visible on RS)
Knit the 2nd st from front of work, knit 1st st and slip both sts from needle

CHART 1

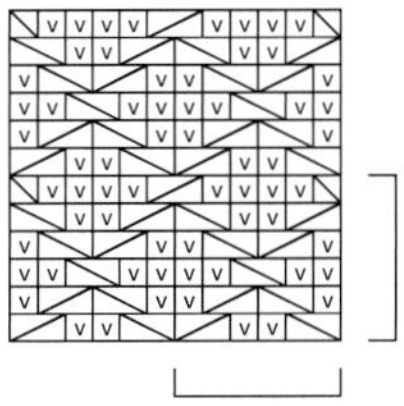

Repeat

Repeat

CHART 2

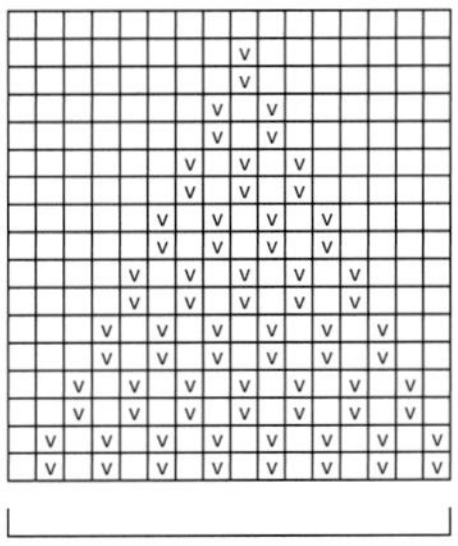

Repeat

CHART 3

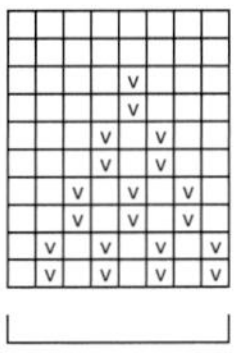

Repeat

Elegant Fana Sweater

Striped sweaters are common all around Norway—both inland and along the coast. We can see examples of them in old paintings and photographs. Striped sweaters were, first and foremost, work garments, and many people think the first knitted striped sweaters in Norway were mass-produced and imported from the Faroe Islands, Iceland, Denmark, or England. After that, we see sweaters beginning to feature block panels on their lower edges, and star panels on sleeve cuffs. Some also had split lower edges with two-end knitting. Such details are not included in sweaters that were imported from abroad; many think these sweaters were knitted here in Norway, by family members.

In Fana (on Norway's west coast), we have been able to document striped sweaters in continual use since the middle of the nineteenth century. There is, for example, a photo of Torbjørn Halldorsen Hop (1825-1899) that was taken between 1860 and 1870. The type of sweater he's wearing, underneath his vest, was common at that time and we can clearly see that it has eight-petal roses on the cuffs.

Around 1900, a number of people began knitting striped sweaters for sale. Members of the Bergen Ski Team bought them, as did Bergen residents who supported dissolution of the union with Sweden in 1905. At the beginning of the 1930s, the Bergen Handcraft Association published a pattern for a Fana sweater, and in 1936-37, Randi Kielland (who had a knitting business in Bergen) also published one. During World War II, interest in Fana patterns grew, both locally and in the rest of the country. Everything that was authentically Norwegian became a symbol of freedom. And when Princess Ragnhild and Erling Lorentzen wore Fana sweaters at the beginning of the 1950s, interest in these garments exploded.

Torbjørn Halldorson Hop with his wife Cesilia J. Nattland and three of their children, photographed by Marcus Selmer between 1860 and 1870.

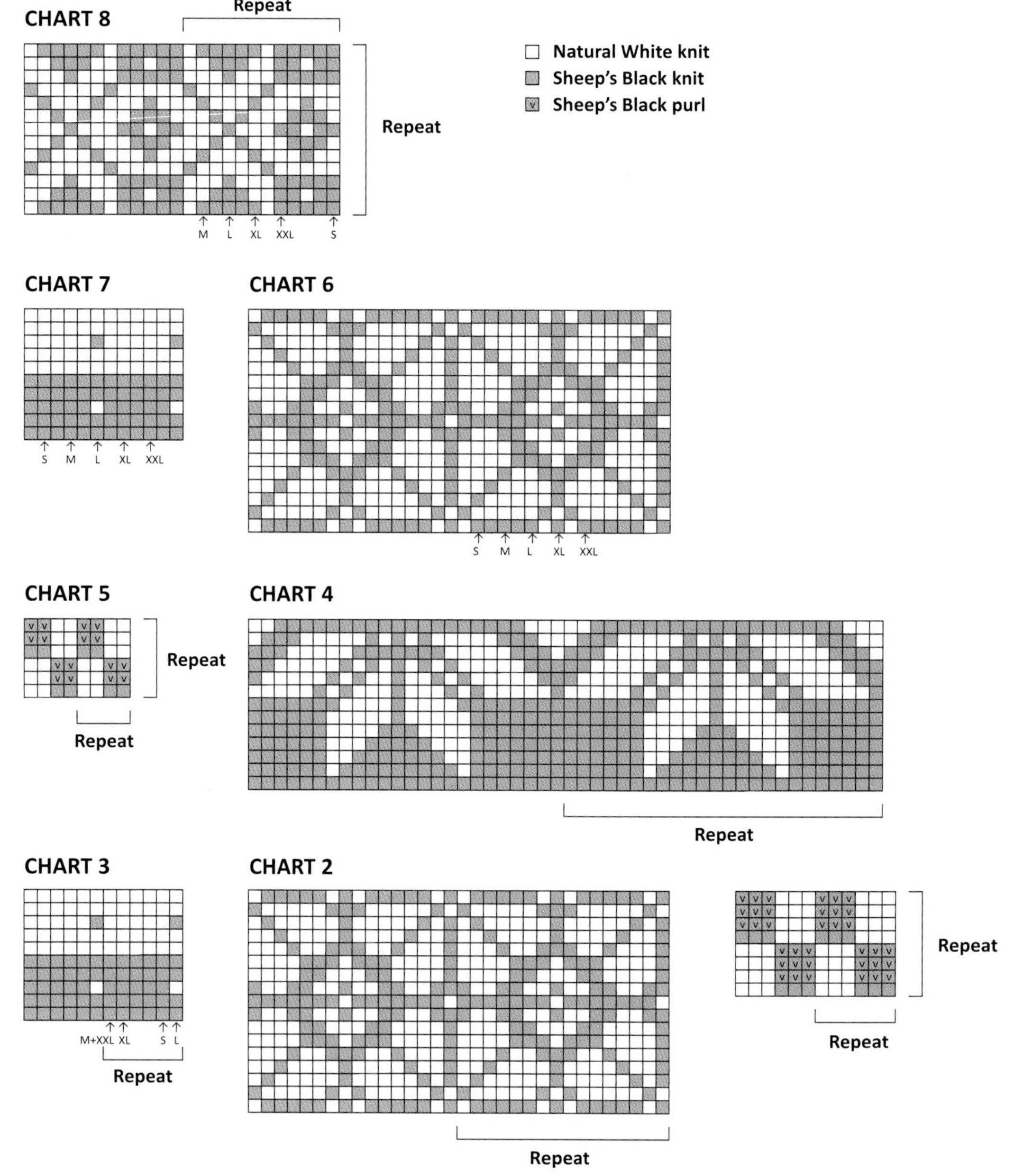

INSTRUCTIONS

Skill Level: Experienced

SIZES
S (M, L, XL, XXL)

FINISHED MEASUREMENTS
Chest: 37½ (39¾, 42½, 45, 47¼) in / 95 (101, 108, 114, 120) cm
Waist: 32¼ (35, 37½, 39¾, 42½) in / 82 (89, 95, 101, 108) cm
Sleeve Length: 18½ (19, 19¼, 19¾, 20) in / 47 (48, 49, 50, 51) cm

Total Length: 18½ (18½, 18½, 19¾, 19¾) in / 47 (47, 47, 50, 50) cm

MATERIALS
Yarn:
CYCA #1 (fingering) Rauma 2-ply Gammelserie (100% Norwegian wool, 175 yd/160 m / 50 g)

Yarn Colors and Amounts:
Natural White 401: 150 (200, 200, 250, 250) g
Sheep's Black 410: 200 (250, 250, 300, 300) g

Needles:
U. S. sizes 1.5 and 2.5 / 2.5 and 3 mm: circulars
and sets of 5 dpn

Crochet Hook:
small size

Notions:
8 buttons

GAUGE
25 sts x 35 rnds = 4 x 4 in / 10 x 10 cm.
Adjust needle size to obtain correct gauge if
necessary.

BODY
With Black and larger circular, CO 206 (222, 238,
254, 270) sts + 5 extra sts for steek (steek sts are
not included in stitch counts; see pages 8 and 12).
Join, being careful not to twist cast-on row; pm
for beginning of rnd. Work block pattern following
Chart 1. Work chart twice in length. Knit 1 rnd
Black, *at the same time* increasing 3 sts evenly
spaced around (do not increase in steek) = 209
(225, 241, 257, 273) sts. Now work panel following Chart 2.
Pm at each side so you'll have 52 (56, 60, 64, 68)
sts for each front and 105 (113, 121, 129, 137) sts
for back. Work in stripes following Chart 3, beginning at arrow for your size. *At the same time*, CO
2 sts at each side on every other stripe a total of
7 times for each front and 6 times on the back =
235 (251, 267, 283, 299) sts. Continue in stripes
until body measures 17¼ (17¼, 17¼, 18½, 18½) in
/ 44 (44, 44, 47, 47) cm. The last stripe should be
in Black.
Now work following Chart 4. Each front should
have 59 (63, 67, 71, 75) sts. When beginning the
back, begin at the same st in the pattern as the
last st on the front. Read the chart from right to
left. When you place the front against the back,
it's important that the patterns match precisely
and are symmetrical for the shoulders.
Turn body inside out. Move sts on the needle so
you can begin at one of the side markers. Join
back and front with 3-needle bind-off: Slip sts for
one shoulder to dpn, with each set on a separate
dpn. Hold the needles parallel, with RS facing RS.
Using a third needle, k2tog with 1 st each from
front and back. *K2tog with next pair of sts and
slip 1st worked st on right needle over 2nd. Rep
from * to steek. Make sure the patterns align. Cut
yarn and draw end through last loop. Join second
shoulder the same way, beginning at marker on
opposite side. When you turn the sweater right
side out, you should have a perfect star panel
over each shoulder. If you prefer, you can join the
shoulders, RS out, with Kitchener st.

SLEEVES
With Black and larger dpn, CO 52 (56, 60, 64,
68) sts. Divide sts onto 4 dpn and join; pm for
beginning of rnd. Work block pattern following
Chart 5. Work chart twice in length. Knit 1 rnd
Black, *at the same time* increasing 1 st centered
on underarm. Now work panel on Chart 6.
Continue in stripes as for body following Chart 7
and beginning at arrow for your size. *At the same
time*, increase 2 sts at center of underarm on
every 6th rnd until you have a total of 89 (93, 97,
101, 105) sts. Continue in pattern until sleeve is
17 (17¼, 17¾, 18¼, 18½) in / 43 (44, 45, 46, 47)
cm long and then work panel of Chart 8. Turn
sleeve inside out and, with Black, knit 6 rnds for
facing. BO loosely.

Make the second sleeve the same way.

FINISHING
Weave in all ends neatly on WS. Trace the neck
opening following template on page 10. Crochet
or machine-baste all around the neckline. Crochet
or machine-stitch the facing along the front steek.
Begin with left front band.
Left Front Band: With Black yarn, pick up and knit
sts (use crochet hook to make it easier). Pick up 3
sts for every 4 sts or rows. With smaller circular,
work back and forth in stockinette for 6 rows,
work eyelet row on WS for foldline: (k2tog, yo)
across. Work 6 more rows in stockinette and then
BO.
Right Front Band: Mark spacing of 8 buttons on
left band. With Black yarn, pick up and knit sts as
for left band (make sure you have the same number of sts). Work back and forth in stockinette.
Make a buttonhole with BO 2 sts opposite each
button marker. On next row, CO 2 sts over each
gap. For foldline, knit eyelet row on WS. Continue
in stockinette, making buttonholes on facing to
match those on outside of band. BO.
Now carefully cut open steek. Sew facings over
cut edges of steek. With Black, sew buttonhole st
all around each buttonhole.
Neckband: With Black and smaller circular, pick
up and knit sts around neck. Work neckband as
for front bands. Fold down and sew facing down
neatly on WS.
Armholes: Measure width of sleeve top and then
mark that length from shoulder down side. Crochet or machine-stitch two lines on each side of
center side st. Cut each armhole open carefully.

Attach sleeves with mattress st on RS. Turn
facings to WS and sew down to cover cut edges.
Gently steam press sweater under a damp pressing cloth. Sew on buttons.

Cropped Vestland Cardigan

At the University Museum in Bergen, you'll see a photograph of a man in a knitted sweater with both stripes with lice and blocks of cross motifs. At first glance, it looks like a cropped sweater, but on closer inspection, you can tell the man has the sweater tucked into his trousers instead. The lower section is white, so we can conclude that it's a nineteenth-century garment.

Striped sweaters can be found almost everywhere in Norway, but stripes with lice are characteristic of Fana sweaters. The block pattern on this sweater is also found in most of Norway. In Fana, it's called a cross pattern; in other places, it's referred to as a clover pattern, among other names. The modest pattern often appears on work clothes but also appeared on mittens. This sweater also has a decorative pattern panel at the top of the sleeves.

CHART 5

CHART 4

CHART 3

CHART 2

CHART 1

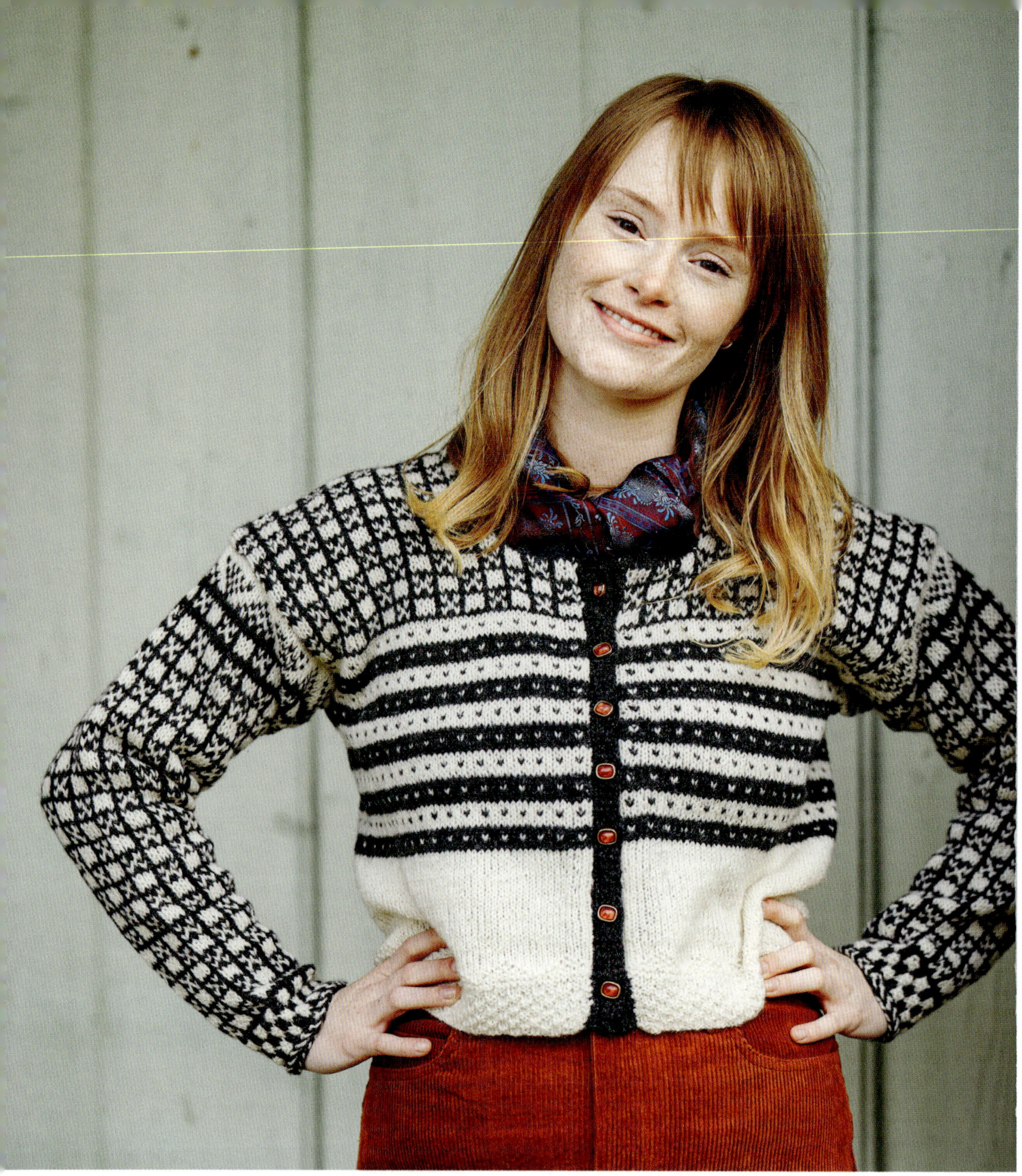

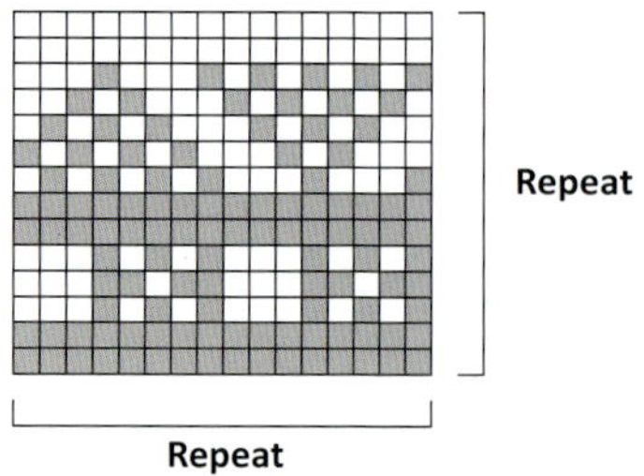

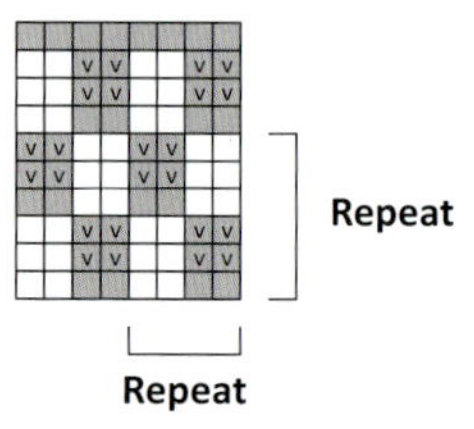

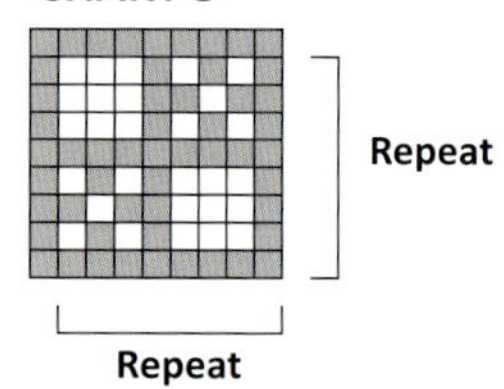

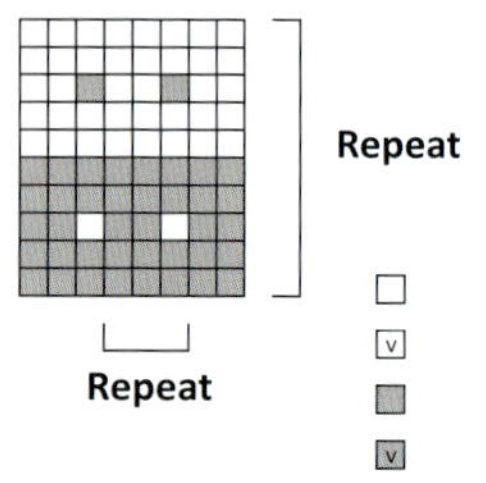

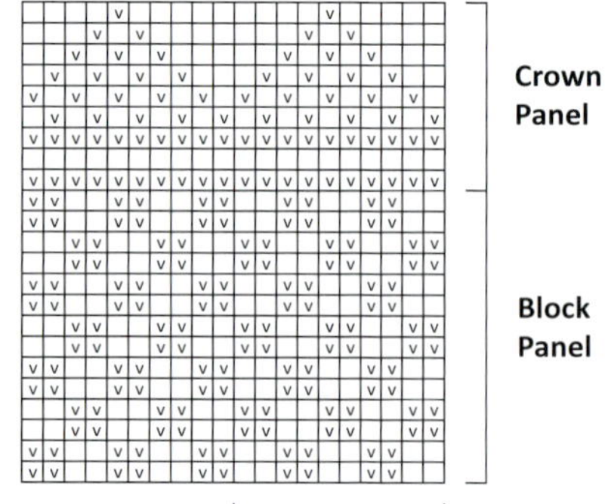

INSTRUCTIONS

Skill Level: Experienced

SIZES
S (M, L, XL, XXL)

FINISHED MEASUREMENTS
Chest: 36¾ (38½, 42¼, 43¾, 47¼) in / 93 (98, 107, 111, 120) cm
Total Length: 17¼ (18¼, 19, 19¾, 20½) in / 44 (46, 48, 50, 52) cm
Sleeve Length: 18¼ (18½ 18½, 19, 19) in / 46 (47, 47, 48, 48) cm

MATERIALS
Yarn:
CYCA #2 (sport, baby) Hillesvåg Ask (100% Norwegian wool, 344 yd/315 m / 100 g)

Yarn Colors and Amounts:
Charcoal Gray 316056: 150 (150, 200, 200, 250) g
Half-bleached White 316047: 200 (250, 250, 300, 300) g

Needles:
U. S. size 2.5 / 3 mm: circular and set of 5 dpn

Crochet Hook:
U. S. size D-3 / 3 mm

Notions:
6 or 7 buttons

GAUGE

23 sts x 29 rnds = 4 x 4 in / 10 x 10 cm. Adjust needle size to obtain correct gauge if necessary.

BODY

With White and circular, CO 211 (221, 241, 251, 271) sts + 6 extra sts for steek (steek sts are not included in stitch counts; see pages 8 and 12). Join, being careful not to twist cast-on row; pm for beginning of rnd. Work checkerboard ribbing and crown panel following Chart 1. Knit around in White until body measures 5¼ in / 13 cm. On the last rnd, adjust st count to 212 (221, 242, 251, 272) sts, evenly spacing around (do not increase in steek).

Now work stripes with lice following Chart 2 until body measures approx. 11¾ (12¼, 12¾, 13, 13½) in / 30 (31, 32, 33, 34) cm. Complete light or dark stripe and, on last rnd, adjust stitch count to 213 (221, 241, 253, 273) sts. Continue with block patterns following Chart 3 until you reach total body length. End with a complete pattern.

Turn body inside out. Join back and front with 3-needle bind-off: Hold the needles parallel, with RS facing RS. Using Charcoal and third needle, k2tog with 1 st each from front and back. *K2tog with next pair of sts and slip 1st worked st on right needle over 2nd. Rep from * to steek. Make sure patterns align. Cut yarn and draw end through last loop. Join second shoulder the same way. When you turn the sweater right side out, you should have a perfect seam over the shoulders. If you prefer, you can join the shoulders, RS out, with Kitchener st.

SLEEVES

With Charcoal and dpn, CO 44 (48, 52, 56, 60) sts. Divide sts onto 4 dpn and join; pm for beginning of rnd. (K1 dark, k1 light) all around. Work 2-end braid as explained on page 15. Work checkerboard ribbing and crown panel following Chart 4. On last rnd, increase 1 st at center of underarm. Continue, working blocks following Chart 3. On the chart, begin with the 5th (1st, 5th, 1st, 5th) st as counted from the right so the pattern will be the same on each side of the center underarm st. *At the same time*, increase 2 sts at center of underarm on every 6th rnd until you have a total of 92 (96, 100, 104, 108) sts.

Continue in pattern until sleeve is 15¾ (16¼, 16¼, 16½, 16½) in / 40 (41, 41, 42, 42) cm long and then work Chart 5. Make sure bottom row of blocks aligns with motifs in previous panel. Turn sleeve inside out and, with White, knit around for ¾ in / 2 cm for facing. BO loosely. Make the second sleeve the same way.

FINISHING

Neckline: The neckline is squared and follows the block patterning. Mark neckline 3 blocks in on each side and 5 blocks high on the front and 2 blocks high on the back. Stitch by hand or machine to outline the neckline. Work single crochet to allow an approx. ⅝ in / 1.5 cm wide facing around the neck. Crochet each straight piece separately for neat corners. Cut away fabric inside neckline stitching. Cover cut edges with facing and sew down on WS.

Armholes: Measure width of sleeve top and then mark that length from shoulder down side. Crochet or machine-stitch two lines on each side of center side st. Cut each armhole open carefully. Attach sleeves with mattress st on RS. Turn facings to WS and sew down to cover cut edges.

Stitch two lines on each side of center steek st. On each side of steek, pick up sts and crochet a facing with single crochet, about ¾ in / 2 cm wide. Carefully cut open steek. Sew facings over cut edges of steek. Make a single crochet band the same length as cardigan front. Sew band to front on left side. Mark spacing for 6 or 7 buttons and make another band with buttonholes spaced as for buttons. For each buttonhole: ch 2, skip 2 sts; on next row, work 2 sc into each ch-loop.

Weave in all ends neatly on WS. Gently steam press sweater under a damp pressing cloth. Sew on buttons.

Old-Fashioned Bergen Pullover

The photographer Knud Knudsen (1832-1915) documented the striped pull-overs worn in the district around Bergen (on Norway's west coast) in the 1860s and 1870s. By 1864, he had already opened a photography studio on Strandgaten ("Beach Street") in Bergen, and he quickly set up himself as a portrait photographer The camera was also with him when he went home to Odda in Hardanger or went off on other trips. His journeys took him up, down, and across Norway, even though carrying the equipment was challenging and transport was hard to arrange. On these tours, he took a number of photos, which captured how widespread various knitting techniques were. Many photos can be dated quite precisely.

One photo from Tysnes, dated 1865-1870, shows a whole group of men and a child in striped sweaters. At first glance, the sweaters all look alike—but the stripes actu-ally have varying widths, and the colors are also a bit different. On the lower edges of the sleeves, we can see that one has crosswise stripes, another has a block panel, and the sweater on the man to the right in the foreground has eight-petal roses. These different pattern elements show the sweaters were locally hand-knit. Imported sweaters didn't have these kinds of details.

"Party from Tysnes Island," photographed by Knud Knudsen between 1865 and 1870.

INSTRUCTIONS

Skill Level: Experienced

SIZES
S (M, L, XL, XXL)

FINISHED MEASUREMENTS
Chest: 38½ (41, 43¼, 45¾, 48) in / 98 (104, 110, 116, 122) cm
Waist: 33 (35½, 37¾, 40¼, 42½) in / 84 (90, 96, 102, 108) cm
Sleeve Length: 17 (17¼, 17¾, 18¼, 18½) in / 43 (44, 45, 46, 47) cm
Total Length: 24½ (25¼, 26, 26¾, 27½) in / 62 (64, 66, 68, 70) cm

MATERIALS
Yarn:
CYCA #2 (sport, baby) Hillesvåg Ask (100% Norwegian wool, 344 yd/315 m / 100 g)

Yarn Colors and Amounts:
Natural White 316057: 200 (200, 200, 250, 250) g
Light Blue-Violet Heather 316541: 150 (200, 200, 250, 250) g

Needles:
U. S. size 4 / 3.5 mm: circular and set of 5 dpn

GAUGE
20 sts x 32 rnds = 4 x 4 in / 10 x 10 cm.
Adjust needle size to obtain correct gauge if necessary.

BODY
With White and circular, CO 168 (180, 192, 204, 216) sts. Join, being careful not to twist cast-on row; pm for beginning of rnd. Work around in k2, p2 ribbing for 2¾ in / 7 cm. After ribbing, work in stockinette until body measures 4¾ (5¼, 5½, 5½, 5½) in / 12 (13, 14, 14, 14) cm. Pm at each side with the same number of sts each for front and back. Increase 2 sts at each side (M1 on each side of each marker). Now work stripe pattern following Chart 1. *At the same time*, increase as before on every 20ᵗʰ rnd a total of 6 times = 192 (204, 216, 228, 240) sts. Continue stripes until body measures 17 (17¼, 17¾, 18¼, 18½) in / 43 (44, 45, 46, 47) cm. Now divide body for front and back and work each separately.

FRONT
Continue stripes, working back and forth in stockinette until piece measures 23¼ (24, 24¾, 25½, 26½) in / 59 (61, 63, 65, 67) cm. Hold work with RS facing you and BO center front for neck: K37 (39, 41, 43, 45), BO the next 22 (24, 26, 28, 30) sts, k33 (35, 37, 39, 41). Leave the last 4 sts on needle or holder.
Now continue shaping neckline *at the same time* as shaping shoulders with short rows. Work the left side first:
Purl back; turn and BO 3 sts, knit until 8 sts rem; turn.
Purl back; turn and BO 2 sts, knit until 12 sts rem; turn.
Purl back; turn and BO 2 sts, knit until 16 sts rem; turn.
Purl back; turn and BO 1 st, knit until 20 sts rem; turn.
Purl back; turn and BO 1 st, knit until 24 sts rem; turn.
Continue the same way until the entire shoulder has been shaped.
Place the 28 (30, 32, 34, 36) shoulder sts on a holder and work the right side the same way, reversing shaping to match. Neckline decreases are worked on the WS.

BACK
Continue stripes, working back and forth in stockinette until piece measures 23¼ (24, 24¾, 25½, 26½) in / 59 (61, 63, 65, 67) cm. Shape shoulders before you begin shaping neck.
Make sure that you begin the same way on both back and front. Work until 4 sts rem; turn.
Purl back; turn when 4 sts rem on the other side; turn.
Knit back; turn when 8 sts rem; turn.
Purl back; turn when 8 sts rem; turn.
Continue the same way until piece measures 23¼ in / 59 cm. *At the same time*, shape neck: BO 22 (24, 26, 28, 30) sts at center back for back neck. At neck edge, BO 3,2,2,1,1 sts as on front neck. Continue until the entire shoulder has been shaped.

When both back and front are finished, turn work inside out with RS facing RS. Place all back sts on one needle and front sts on another needle (or on the other tip of a circular).

Using either color and third needle, k2tog with 1 st each from front and back (make sure you join same color sts). *K2tog with next pair of sts and slip 1ˢᵗ worked st on right needle over 2ⁿᵈ. Rep from * until all sts have been bound off.
Make sure patterns align. Cut yarn and draw end through last loop. Join second shoulder the same way.

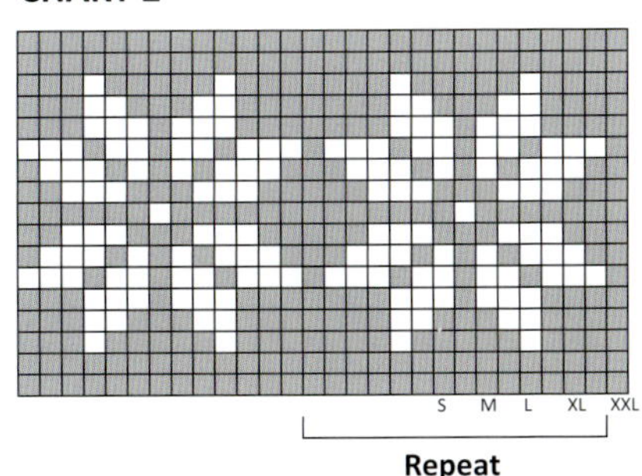

SLEEVES

With Blue-Violet and dpn, CO 41 (45, 49, 53, 57) sts. Divide sts onto 4 dpn and join; pm for beginning of rnd. Knit 2 rnds. Make an eyelet foldline: (k2tog, yo) around. Now work star pattern following Chart 2. After star panel, work in stripes following Chart 3. *At the same time*, M1 before and after center underarm st on every 5th rnd until there are 75 sts. Next, increase on every 6th rnd until there are a total of 83 (87, 91, 95, 99) sts. Continue in stripes until sleeve measures 17 (17¼, 17¾, 18¼, 18½) in / 43 (44, 45, 46, 47) cm. BO. Make the second sleeve the same way.

FINISHING

With Blue-Violet and circular, pick up and knit sts around neck (use a crochet hook to pick up sts if necessary). Purl 1 rnd, knit 4 rnds, purl 1 rnd (foldline), knit 4 rnds. BO (make sure bind-off is not too tight).

Attach sleeves with RS facing and mattress st. Fold edging on sleeve cuffs at eyelet rnd and sew down on WS. Weave in all ends neatly on WS. Gently steam press sweater under a damp pressing cloth.

Bergen Pullover with Star Panels

Marcus Selmer (1819-1900) was the first photographer to become established in Bergen. He came from Denmark, and most likely started as early as 1852. *Bergen boys from Glæsvær* is a photo from the series "Norwegian National Costumes," which was published in 1872. Most of the photos in this series were taken in Selmer's studio, but this particular photo was taken outside. We can see fishing lines in the background. You can also see a hint of "lens flare" between the boys.

The two boys, both from the fishery west of Bergen, wore striped sweaters under their vests and jackets. The boy on the right is wearing a striped sweater with a block pattern on the lower edge. Between his trousers and vest, we know the sweater has a light single-color section. He also has a multi-color pattern-knitted hat on his head. This photo was hand-colored, so we have a good impression of the colors. We can't see any similar pattern elements in the clothing of the boy on the left. Both have thick felted stockings on their legs and wooden shoes on their feet. This photo inspired me to make a striped pullover with pattern panels.

Bergen boys from Glæsvær *from the series "Norwegian National Costumes," 1866- 1867.*

CHART 1

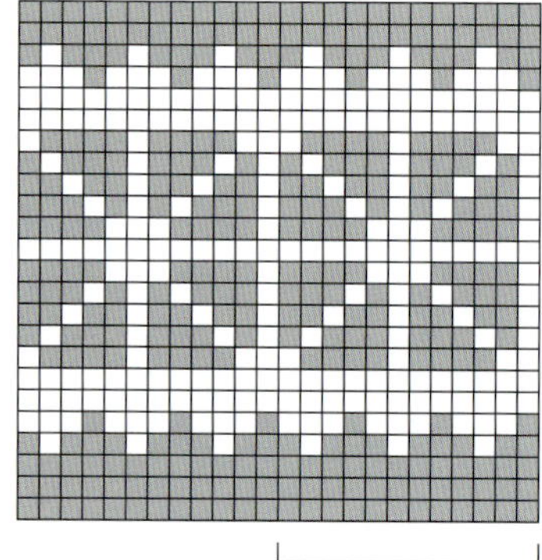

CHART 3

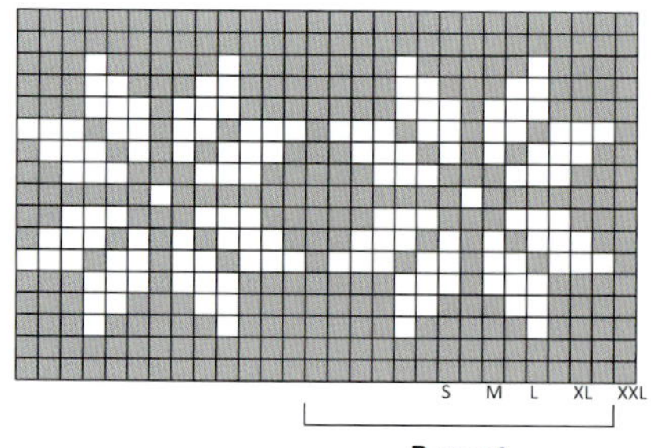

CHART 2

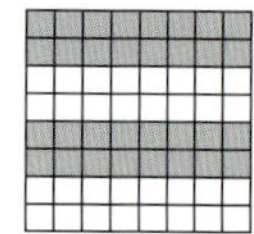

INSTRUCTIONS

Skill Level: Experienced

SIZES
S (M, L, XL, XXL)

FINISHED MEASUREMENTS
Chest: 38½ (41, 43¼, 45¾, 48) in / 98 (104, 110, 116, 122) cm
Waist: 33 (35½, 37¾, 40¼, 42½) in / 84 (90, 96, 102, 108) cm
Sleeve Length: 17 (17¼, 17¾, 18¼, 18½) in / 43 (44, 45, 46, 47) cm
Total Length: 24½ (25¼, 26, 26¾, 27½) in / 62 (64, 66, 68, 70) cm

MATERIALS
Yarn:
CYCA #2 (sport, baby) Hillesvåg Ask (100% Norwegian wool, 344 yd/315 m / 100 g)

Yarn Colors and Amounts:
Natural White 316057: 150 (200, 200, 250, 250) g
Light Blue-Violet Heather 316541: 150 (200, 200, 250, 250) g

Needles:
U. S. size 4 / 3.5 mm: circular and set of 5 dpn

GAUGE

20 sts x 32 rnds = 4 x 4 in / 10 x 10 cm.
Adjust needle size to obtain correct gauge if
necessary.

BODY

With Blue-Violet and circular, CO 168 (180,
192, 204, 216) sts. Join, being careful not to
twist cast-on row; pm for beginning of rnd.
Knit 4 rnds. Purl 1 rnd for foldline. Work in
pattern following Chart 1. Pm at each side
with the same number of sts each for front
and back. Increase 2 sts at each side (M1 on
each side of each marker). Continue in stripe
pattern following Chart 2 and, *at the same
time*, increase as before on every 20th rnd a
total of 6 times = 192 (204, 216, 228, 240) sts.
Continue stripes until body measures 17 (17¼,
17¾, 18¼, 18½) in / 43 (44, 45, 46, 47) cm.
Now divide body for front and back and work
each separately.

FRONT

Continue stripes, working back and forth in
stockinette until piece measures 23¼ (24, 24¾,
25½, 26½) in / 59 (61, 63, 65, 67) cm. Hold
work with RS facing you and BO center front
for neck: K37 (39, 41, 43, 45), BO the next 22
(24, 26, 28, 30) sts, k33 (35, 37, 39, 41). Leave
the last 4 sts on needle or holder.
Now continue shaping neckline, *at the same
time* as shaping shoulders with short rows.
Work the left side first:
Purl back; turn and BO 3 sts, knit until 8 sts
rem; turn.
Purl back; turn and BO 2 sts, knit until 12 sts
rem; turn.
Purl back; turn and BO 2 sts, knit until 16 sts
rem; turn.
Purl back; turn and BO 1 st, knit until 20 sts
rem; turn.
Purl back; turn and BO 1 st, knit until 24 sts
rem; turn.
Continue the same way until the entire shoulder has been shaped.
Place the 28 (30, 32, 34, 36) shoulder sts on
a holder and work the right side the same
way, reversing shaping to match. Neckline
decreases are worked on the WS.

BACK

Continue stripes, working back and forth in
stockinette until piece measures 23¼ (24, 24¾,
25½, 26½) in / 59 (61, 63, 65, 67) cm. Shape
neck and shoulders as for front.

on front neck. Continue until the entire shoulder has been shaped.

When both back and front are finished, turn
work inside out with RS facing RS. Place
all back sts on one needle and front sts on
another needle (or on the other tip of a
circular).
   Using either color and a third needle, begin
at outer edge of shoulder; k2tog with 1 st each
from front and back (make sure you join same
color sts). *K2tog with next pair of sts and pass
1st worked st on right needle over 2nd. Rep
from * until all sts have been bound off. Make
sure patterns/colors align. Cut yarn and draw
end through last loop. Join second shoulder
the same way.

SLEEVES

With Blue-Violet and dpn, CO 41 (45, 49, 53,
57) sts. Divide sts onto 4 dpn and join; pm for
beginning of rnd. Knit 2 rnds. Make an eyelet
foldline: (k2tog, yo) around. Now work star
pattern following Chart 3. After star panel,
work in stripes following Chart 2. *At the same
time*, M1 before and after center underarm st
on every 5th rnd until there are 67 (71, 75, 79,
83) sts. Next, increase on every 6th rnd until
there are a total of 83 (87, 91, 95, 99). Continue in stripes until sleeve measures approx.
13¾ (13¾, 13¾, 14½, 14½) in / 35 (35, 35, 37,
37) cm from foldline (the last stripe should be
White). Work following Chart 1. Continue with
Blue only until sleeve measures 17 (17¼, 17¾,
18¼, 18½) in / 43 (44, 45, 46, 47) cm. BO.

Make the second sleeve the same way.

FINISHING

With Blue-Violet and circular, pick up and knit
sts around neck (use a crochet hook to pick up
sts if necessary). Purl 1 rnd, knit 4 rnds, purl
1 rnd (foldline), knit 4 rnds. BO (make sure
bind-off is not too tight). Attach sleeves with
RS facing and mattress st.

Fold edging on sleeve cuffs at eyelet rnd and
sew down on WS. Weave in all ends neatly on
WS. Gently steam press sweater under a damp
pressing cloth.

Green Dress

Knitted sweaters in red or green, and sometimes blue or black, were very common in many places in Norway up until about 1900. These garments were referred to as "night sweaters," although they weren't exclusively nightwear. Hans Strøm wrote that one such sweater could cost as much as three to five riksdaler in 1754—almost as much as an entire year's earnings for a maid servant on Østlandet, at the time. He therefore praised girls who began knitting sweaters themselves instead importing them from England. In order to hinder business from abroad, women were criticized for squandering money on textiles and strongly advised that regular people should wear homemade clothing. Creating an expectation that everyone would use Norwegian raw materials and knit their own sweaters was very good for the Norwegian economy.

Handknitted green sweaters with a rounded neckline were especially common in the outer parts of Hordaland. These sweaters were closely fitted and worn under the bodice instead of a shirt, so long as the weather was cold. It was said that in Austevoll, women might wear several sweaters one on top of the other—a blue one, a green one, and a red one—as a sign of wealth. Others knitted stripes in several colors on their sleeve cuffs, so it would look like they had on several layers of sweaters.

This dress was inspired by the green sweaters of Hordaland. I added pattern panels from a vintage men's sweater from Sotra to the lower edges of the dress and sleeves.

Girl from Onarheim, Tysnæs, from the series "Norwegian National Costumes" from 1866-1867.

☐ Green
☐ Black

CHART 1

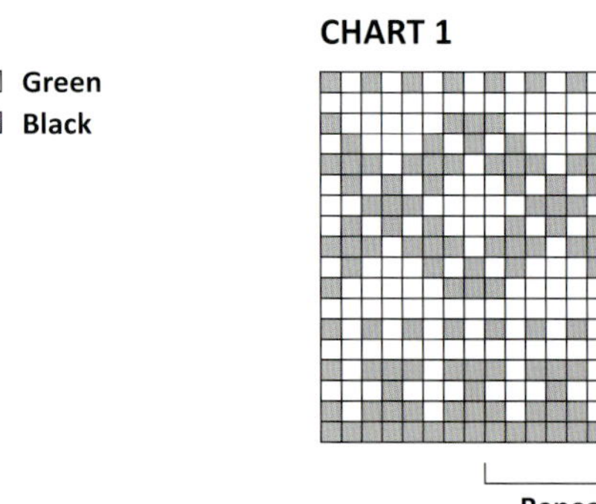

CHART 2

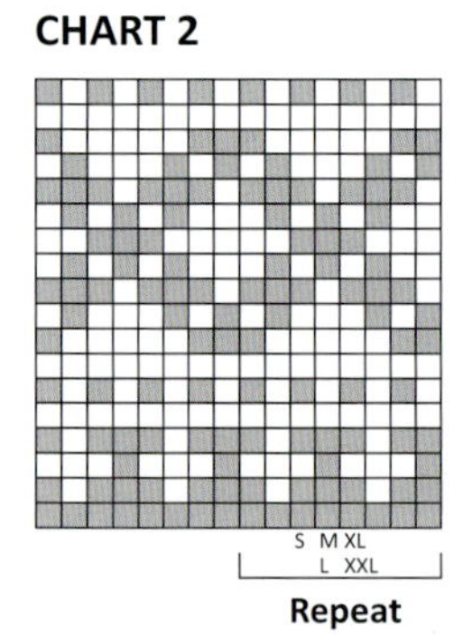

INSTRUCTIONS

Skill Level: Intermediate-Experienced

SIZES
S (M, L, XL, XXL)

FINISHED MEASUREMENTS
Chest: 38½ (41, 45¼, 48¾, 50¾) in / 98 (104, 115, 124, 133) cm
Waist: 36¾ (39½, 43¾, 47¼, 42½) in / 93 (100, 111, 120, 129) cm
Sleeve Length: 13 (13½, 13¾, 14¼, 14½) in / 33 (34, 35, 36, 37) cm
Total Length: 36 (36¾, 37½, 38¼, 39) in / 91 (93, 95, 97, 99) cm

MATERIALS
Yarn:
CYCA #3 (DK, light worsted) Hillesvåg Tinde pelsull-garn (100% Norwegian wool, 284 yd/ 260 m / 100 g)

Yarn Colors and Amounts:
Grass Green 652134: 300 (300, 350, 400, 450) g
Black 652109: 100 (100, 150, 200, 200) g

Needles:
U. S. size 6 / 4 mm: circular and set of 5 dpn

GAUGE
18 sts x 28 rnds = 4 x 4 in / 10 x 10 cm.
Adjust needle size to obtain correct gauge if necessary.

SKIRT
With Black and circular, CO 204 (220, 236, 252, 268) sts. Join, being careful not to twist cast-on row; pm for beginning of rnd. Work block pattern as follows:
X *K2, p2*; rep * to * around for 3 rnds.
P2, k2; rep * to * around for 3 rnds X. Rep X to X 3 times.
Knit 1 rnd, increasing evenly spaced around to 208 (224, 240, 256, 272) sts, and then work in pattern following Chart 1. After completing charted rows, continue in Green until piece measures 16¼ (16½, 17, 17¼, 17¾) in / 41 (42, 43, 44, 45) cm. Pm after 26 (28, 30, 32, 34) sts, pm after 52 (56, 60, 64, 68) sts, pm after another 52 (56, 60, 64, 68) sts, and pm after a 3rd set of 52 (56, 60, 64, 68) sts.
Decrease Rnd: Decrease 2 sts at each marker as follows:*Knit until 3 sts before marker, sl 1, k1, psso, k2, k2tog*; rep * to * at each marker = 8 sts decreased. (Knit 10 rnds; work decrease rnd) 4 more times = 168 (184, 200, 216, 233) sts rem.
Knit without decreasing for 4 in / 10 cm. Now increase 2 sts at each marker on the front only:

Increase Rnd: Knit until 1 st before front marker, *M1, k2, M1*; rep * to * at next front marker. Knit 10 rnds and then work increase rnd once more = 8 sts increased for 176 (192, 208, 224, 240) sts total.
Continue knitting around without shaping until dress measures 28 (28¼, 28¾, 29¼, 29½) in / 71 (72, 73, 74, 75) cm. Pm at each side so you have 92 (100, 108, 116, 124) sts on the front and 84 (92, 100, 108, 116) sts on back. BO 5 sts on each side of each side marker. Set piece aside while you knit sleeves.

SLEEVES
With Black and dpn, CO 46 (48, 48, 50, 50) sts. Divide sts onto 4 dpn and join; pm for beginning of rnd. Work around in k2, p2 ribbing for 2½ in / 6 cm. M1 at beginning of next rnd and work pattern following Chart 2. *At the same time*, increase 2 sts centered on underarm every 6th rnd. After completing charted rows, continue with Green only and sleeve shaping. When sleeve has 71 (75, 75, 79, 79) sts stop increasing and continue until sleeve measures 13 (13½, 13¾, 14¼, 14½) in / 33 (34, 35, 36, 37) cm. On the last rnd, BO 10 sts centered on underarm.

Make second sleeve the same way.

RAGLAN SHAPING
Arrange sleeves and body on circular; pm at each intersection of sleeve and body = 278 (302, 318, 342, 358) sts. Knit 1 rnd with Green. On the next rnd, begin decreasing at each side of each marker as follows: Knit until 3 sts rem before marker, k2tog, k2, sl 1, k1, psso.
Knit 1 rnd. Decrease the same way on *every other* rnd until body measures approx. 33 (34, 34¾, 35½, 36¼) in / 84 (86, 88, 90, 92) cm. On the same rnd as raglan decreases, BO 14 (16, 18, 20, 22) sts at center front for neck. Now work back and forth. BO 3,3,2,2,1 sts at beginning of every row *at the same time* as you continue the raglan shaping at each marker on RS rows.

NECKBAND
With Green, pick up and knit in each of the bound-off sts around neck. Change to Black at one junction of one sleeve and back. Knit 1 rnd, work 6 rnds k2, p2 ribbing and then purl 1 rnd. Work 5 rnds k2, p2 ribbing and then BO in ribbing.

FINISHING
Fold neckband at purl rnd and sew down on WS, covering decrease edge. Seam underarms. Weave in all ends neatly on WS. Gently steam press dress under a damp pressing cloth.

Lurve Cardigan from Nordfjord

The Nordfjord Folk Museum has a garment called the "tattered (*lurve*) sweater." It's called that because it was so tattered when the museum first received it that the pieces barely held together. It wasn't given a registration number, and there was no information given about its owner or origin.

The pattern, done in natural sheep's white and black, is an all-over design and is easy to knit. It consists of dark diagonal triangles inside light blocks, and light triangles inside dark blocks. These can perceived as vertical, horizontal, or diagonal stripes, but if you look very closely and stare at the pattern elements, you can also see dark or light eight-petal roses. The neck is squared, which is characteristic of band sweaters from the region, and directly below the neck is a block with embroidered initials—possibly AISAA. On the sleeve cuffs, you can see a narrow panel with Andrew crosses. Such crosses symbolized victory and salvation. Eight-petal roses were signs for good luck and a symbol of Jesus' resurrection and victory.

A sweater with the same pattern but knitted in green and black wool yarn is in private ownership. That sweater was knitted with finer yarn and smaller needles. It has the initials AMSA on the chest. An earlier owner might have been a farmer from Hornindal. The lower edges of the sleeves have black and red twisted cords. This sweater was darned and mended repeatedly, but overall it's in better shape than the museum's "tattered sweater."

Knitted sweaters were very common as Sunday garments for men in Nordfjord in the nineteenth century—particularly between 1840 and 1860. However, knitted sweaters weren't worn in church, nor when it was very warm. Under a sweater, men usually wore a shirt or half-shirt with white embroidery and silver buttons at the neck. A double-breasted vest could be worn over the sweater. Over all that, the men might also wear a jacket called a *jigg*. In total, this outfit was essentially a folk version of the dress coat and tails that were fashionable at the end of the 1700s.

CHART 1

Repeat

Repeat

CHART 2

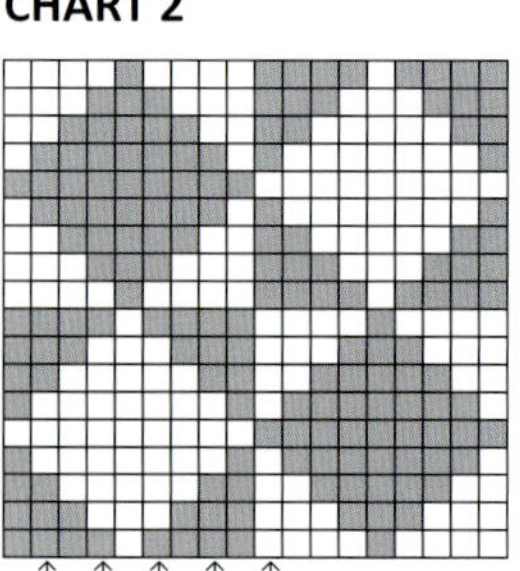

INSTRUCTIONS

Skill Level: Intermediate-Experienced

SIZES
S (M, L, XL, XXL)

FINISHED MEASUREMENTS
Chest: 38¼ (41, 44, 47, 49¾) in / 97 (104, 112, 119, 126) cm
Sleeve Length: 17¾ (17¾, 18¼, 18½, 19) in / 45 (45, 46, 47, 48) cm
Total Length: 22¾ (23¾, 24½, 25¼, 26) in / 58 (60, 62, 64, 66) cm

MATERIALS
Yarn:
CYCA #1 (fingering) Hillesvåg ullvarefabrikk Vilje lamullgarn (100% Norwegian lamb's wool, 410 yd/375 m / 100 g)

Yarn Colors and Amounts:
Red 57406: 50 (50, 50, 100, 100) g
Natural White 57400: 150 (150, 200, 200, 250) g
Red-Orange 57405: 150 (150, 200, 200, 250) g

Needles:

U. S. sizes 2.5 and 4 / 3 and 3.5 mm: circulars and sets of 5 dpn

Notions:

8 buttons

GAUGE

25 sts x 27 rnds = 4 x 4 in / 10 x 10 cm. Adjust needle size to obtain correct gauge if necessary.

BODY

With Red and smaller circular, CO 246 (262, 282, 298, 318) sts. Work back and forth as follows: K1, *p2, k2* to last st and end k1. Turn and work sts as they face you. Rep these 2 rows until ribbing measures 2¾ in / 7 cm. Change to Red-Orange and larger circular. At beginning of row, CO 5 sts for steek (see pages 8 and 12, steek sts are not included in stitch counts). Join and knit 1 rnd, decreasing evenly spaced around to 243 (261, 279, 297, 315) sts. Pm at each side with 60 (65, 69, 74, 78) sts for each front and 123 (131, 141, 149, 159) sts for back.

Now work in pattern following Chart 1. The repeat is 36 sts and 36 rows but individual blocks are 9 sts x 9 rows. Continue as est until body measures 22¾ (23¾, 24½, 25¼, 26) in / 58 (60, 62, 64, 66) cm. Set body aside. If you want the pattern on body and sleeves to match, you must end in the middle of a repeat over 9 sts or on the 5th pattern row.

Turn work inside out. Arrange so you can begin at a side marker. Join front and back with 3-needle bind-off. With any color and a third needle, begin at side; k2tog with 1 st each from front and back (make sure you join same color sts). *K2tog with next pair of sts and pass 1st worked st on right needle over second. Rep from * until all sts to steek have been bound off. Make sure patterns align. Cut yarn and draw end through last loop. Join second shoulder the same way. Alternatively, you can join the shoulders with Kitchener st with right sides facing out.

SLEEVES

With Red and smaller dpn, CO 48 (52, 56, 60, 64) sts. Divide sts onto dpn and join. Work around in k2, p2 ribbing for 2¾ in / 7 cm. On the last rnd, M1 at beginning of rnd. Change to larger dpn. Beginning at arrow for your size

on Chart 2, work in pattern. *At the same time,* increase 2 sts centered on underarm on every 4th rnd, with 1 st, then 3, 5, etc between new sts until there are 95 (99, 105, 109,115) sts. When sleeve is 16½ (16½, 17, 17¼, 17¾) in / 42 (42, 43, 44, 45) cm long, begin an under-arm gusset by adding 2 sts on every other rnd. Continue in pattern until sleeve measures 17¾ (17¾, 18¼, 18½, 19) in / 45 (45, 46, 47, 48) cm. Turn sleeve inside out and knit 5 rnds for a facing. BO loosely. Make the second sleeve the same way.

FINISHING

Weave in all ends neatly on WS. Trace the neck opening following template on page 10. Crochet or machine-baste all around the neckline. Crochet or machine-stitch to reinforce steek edges.

Left Front Band: With Red yarn, pick up and knit sts 3 sts for every 4 rows (use crochet hook to make it easier). With smaller circular, work back and forth in k2, p2 ribbing for 1¼ in / 3 cm. BO in ribbing.

Right Front Band: Mark spacing of 8 buttons on left band. With Red, pick up and knit sts as for left band (make sure you have the same number of sts). Work back and forth in k2, p2 ribbing. When band is about ⅝ in / 1.5 cm wide, make buttonholes. Make a buttonhole with BO 2 sts opposite each button marker. On next row, CO 2 sts over each gap. Continue in ribbing until band is 1¼ in / 3 cm wide. BO in ribbing.

Now carefully cut open steek. Fold steek to WS and sew down neatly or cover with a crocheted facing or ribbon. Optional: With Red, sew buttonhole st all around each buttonhole.

Neckband: With Red and smaller circular, pick up and knit sts around neck. Work around in k2, p2 ribbing for 1¼ in 3 cm. Purl 1 rnd (foldline) and then work in k2, p2 ribbing for 1¼ in / 3 cm. BO in ribbing. Turn at foldline and sew facing down neatly on WS.

Armholes: Measure width of sleeve top and then mark that length from shoulder down side. Crochet or machine-stitch two lines on each side of center side st. Cut each armhole open carefully.

Attach sleeves with mattress st on RS. Turn facings to WS and sew down to cover cut edges. Gently steam press sweater under a damp pressing cloth. Sew on buttons.

Mittens from Nordmøre

We have a tendency to call every mitten knitted in black and white a Selbu mitten. Very often, museum catalogues all around Norway will list mittens like this as "Selbu mittens" even if they are locally-designed mittens. The Nordmøre Museum Foundation has, for example, a pair of mittens that likely came from Henrik August Dørge (1870-1937), who was district physician in Rindal from 1897 until 1923. He had a large collection of antiques; his daughter Borghild Dørge Johannesen inherited it. When Håkon Dørge Hveding inherited the house from Borghild—who was his grandmother's sister—among the items that the Dørge family donated to the museum was a pair of black and white mittens knitted with fine yarn.

The mittens have three eight-petal roses on the back of the hand and small edged blocks on the sides of the top and small blocks with crosses on the palms, but they also feature the characteristic bands between the inside and outside that we always find on Selbu mittens. However, the tops are also a little different. The ribbing, knitted on later, is short. Eight-petal roses have been knitted all over Europe and throughout Norway and aren't exclusively characteristic of Selbu.

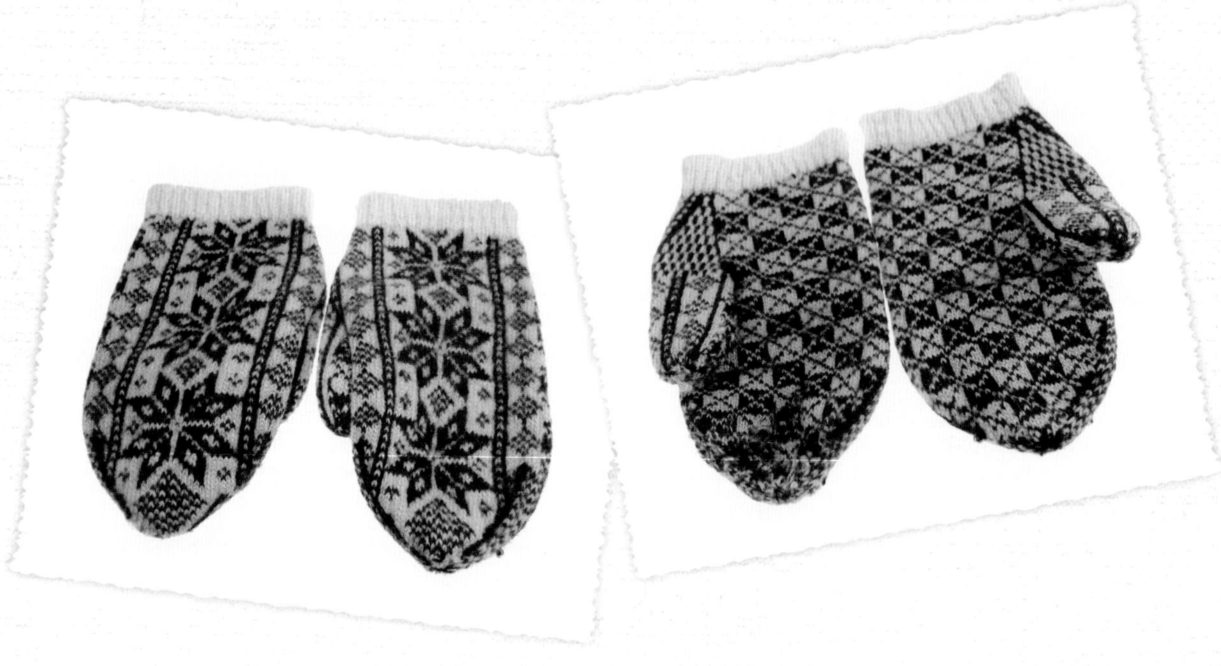

CHART 1

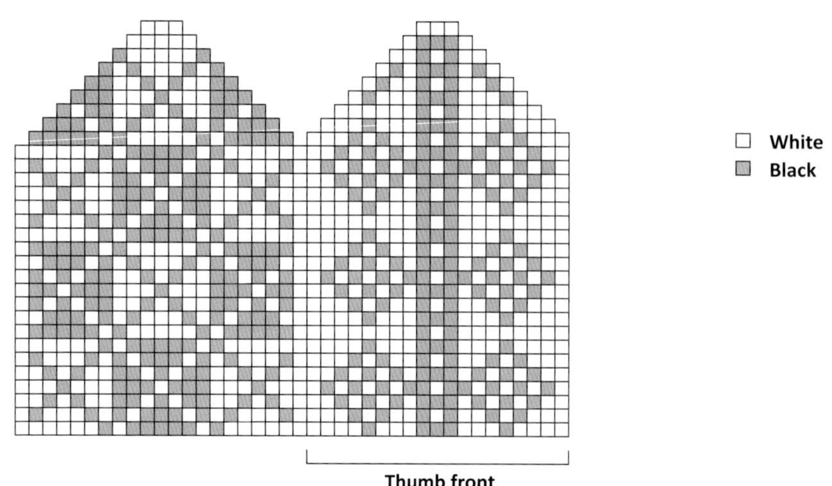

CHART 2: THUMB

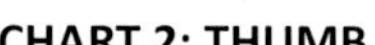

INSTRUCTIONS

Skill Level: Intermediate

SIZES
Women's (Men's)

MATERIALS
Yarn:
CYCA #1 (fingering) Rauma 2-ply Gammelserie
(100% Norwegian wool, 175 yd/160 m / 50 g)

Yarn Colors and Amounts:
White 401: 50 (100) g
Black 436: 50 (100) g

Needles:
U. S. size 0 (1.5) / 2 (2.5) mm: set of 5 dpn

GAUGE
The size is adjusted by changing the gauge/
needle size. Follow the same instructions for
both sizes.
34 (31) sts = 4 in / 10 cm.
Adjust needle size to obtain correct gauge if
necessary.

RIGHT MITTEN
With Black, CO 70 sts. Divide sts evenly onto
4 dpn and join; pm for beginning of rnd. Work
around in k1, p1 ribbing for 1½ in / 4 cm.
On the last rnd, increase 1 st in last st = 71
sts. Now work in pattern following Chart 1.
Increase for thumb gusset as shown on chart.
After working gusset increases, place 19 sts on
a holder for thumb. CO 15 new sts over gap on
next rnd and continue following chart. Shape
top as shown on chart. Cut yarn and draw end
through rem sts; tighten.

THUMB
Pick up and knit 19 + 1 sts for front + 16 sts
over back of thumb. Divide sts onto dpn. On
the next rnd, increase 4 sts over back of thumb
so you have a total of 40 sts around. Work
thumb following Chart 2. Cut yarn and draw
end through rem sts; tighten.

LEFT MITTEN
Work as for right mitten, reversing chart so
thumb is on left side of palm.

FINISHING
Weave in all ends neatly on WS. Wash mittens
gently in lukewarm water and wool-safe soap.
Lay flat and leave until completely dry.

Trønder Star Mittens

"Spit balls" is the name of a pattern that is much used for palms on Selbu mittens. It's the official name for the motif, according to the Selbu Association, because the pattern was inspired by the traces that are left in the snow when drivers spit out chewing tobacco or snuff. Put that way, it doesn't sound very appealing—but this star-shaped pattern is striking, and is found in many different sizes and variations.

I've used it all over the mitten, which breaks with Selbu tradition (on a "true" Selbu mitten, it would be used on the palm, but not the back of the hand). Two-end knitting braids and block panel cuffs also don't belong to the mitten traditions of Selbu.

INSTRUCTIONS

Skill Level: Intermediate

SIZES
Women's (Men's)

MATERIALS
Yarn:
CYCA #3 (DK, light worsted) Rauma 3-ply Strik-kegarn (100% Norwegian wool, 118 yd/108m / 50 g)

Yarn Colors and Amounts:
White 101: 100 (100) g
Light Blue 151: 100 (100) g

Needles:
U. S. size 4 (6) / 3.5 (4) mm: set of 5 dpn

GAUGE
The size is adjusted by changing the gauge/needle size. Follow the same instructions for both sizes.
23 (21) sts = 4 in / 10 cm.
Adjust needle size to obtain correct gauge if necessary.

RIGHT MITTEN
With Blue, CO 48 sts. Divide sts evenly onto 4 dpn and join; pm for beginning of rnd. Work a purl two-end braid (see details on page 15). Work block pattern following Chart 1 and then make another purl two-end braid. Knit 1 rnd with Blue, *at the same time* increasing 2 sts evenly spaced around = 50 sts. Now work in stockinette and pattern following Chart 2. Increase for thumb gusset as shown on chart. After working gusset increases, set aside 9 sts for thumb (see page 14) and continue, following chart. Shape top as shown on chart. Cut yarn and draw end through rem sts; tighten.

THUMB
With White, pick up and knit 11 + 11 sts for thumb. Divide the 22 sts onto dpn. Work thumb in stockinette with White following Chart 3. Lengthen thumb if necessary. Cut yarn and draw end through rem sts; tighten.

LEFT MITTEN
Work as for right mitten, reversing chart so thumb is on left side of palm.

FINISHING
Weave in all ends neatly on WS. Lightly steam press mittens under a damp pressing cloth. If necessary, lightly felt to desired size.

CHART 2

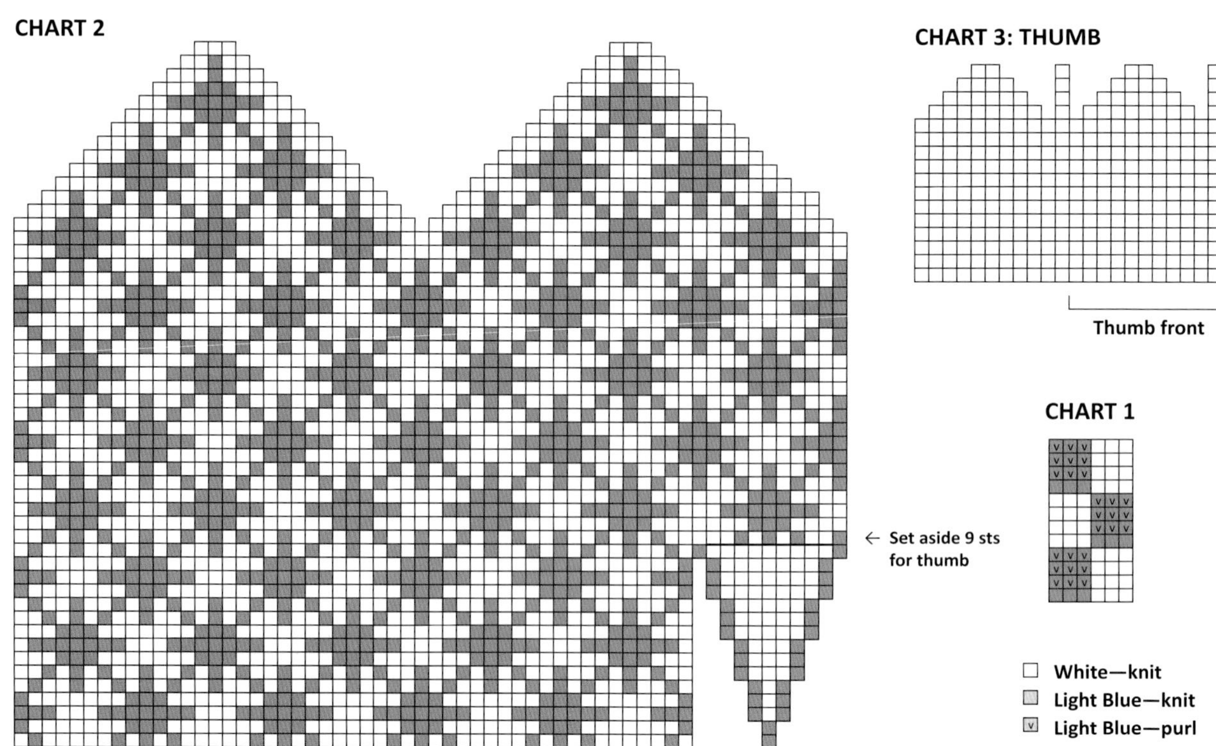

Baby Mittens

Skill Level: Intermediate

SIZES
3 (6, 12) months

MATERIALS
Yarn:
CYCA #3 (DK, light worsted) Rauma 3-ply Strikkegarn (100% Norwegian wool, 118 yd/108m / 50 g)

Yarn Colors and Amounts:
White 101: 50 (50) g
Light Blue 151: 50 (50) g

Needles:
U. S. size 2.5 (4, 6) / 3 (3.5, 4) mm: set of 5 dpn

GAUGE
The size is adjusted by changing the gauge/needle size. Follow the same instructions for both sizes.
25 (23, 21) sts = 4 in / 10 cm.
Adjust needle size to obtain correct gauge if necessary.

RIGHT MITTEN
With Blue, CO 30 sts. Divide sts evenly onto 4 dpn and join; pm for beginning of rnd. Work a purl two-end braid (see details on page 15). Work block pattern following Chart 1. Make an eyelet rnd with Blue: (k2tog, yo) around. Continue, following Chart 2. Shape top as shown on chart. Cut yarn and draw end through rem sts; tighten.

I-CORD
CO 3 sts with White or Blue and work as described on page 12 until cord is about 11¾ in / 30 cm long. Make a second cord the same way. You can make braided or twisted cords instead if you prefer.

LEFT MITTEN
Work as for right mitten.

FINISHING
Weave in all ends neatly on WS. Lightly steam press mittens under a damp pressing cloth. If necessary, felt to desired size.

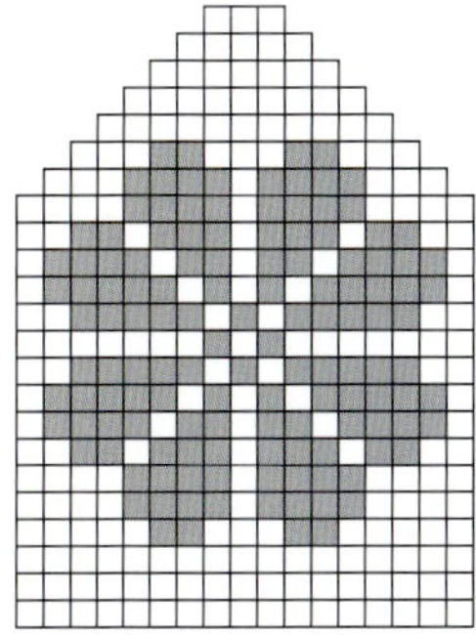

CHART 2

CHART 1

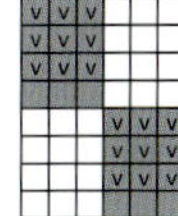

Rose Mittens from Selbu

More than 500 different mitten patterns from Selbu have been collected and registered. No other place in Norway has such a rich and varied pattern tradition. The rules for how Selbu mittens should be knitted were fairly strict, but despite those limitations, there's an enormous amount of variation.

The classic Selbu mitten is constructed differently for women's and men's versions. Generally speaking, women's Selbu mittens have regular ribbed cuffs or lace pattern cuffs, often embellished with simple stripes. Men's Selbu mittens always have a decorative panel for the cuff. The rose mittens described here, therefore, are technically designed like men's mittens. (If you want to hold to tradition and knit them as women's mittens, substitute a ribbed cuff for the leafy vine panel.)

However, all Selbu mittens have a large pattern on the back of the hand, and a simpler and smaller pattern on the palm. A band always rounds the edge of the hand between these two patterns. Both mitten hand and thumb are shaped with a pointed tip. Most Selbu mittens have black patterning on a white background, but there are also black mittens with white patterns, and mittens dyed after knitting to make them black and red.

You will find many variations of the eight-petal rose on mittens from Selbu, and these designs are often called Selbu roses. This variation is particularly decorative with swirls at the outer edges. Locally these swirls are referred to as "goat's horn"—or "billy goat horn"—roses.

CHART 2

Set aside 19 sts
for thumb

CHART 1

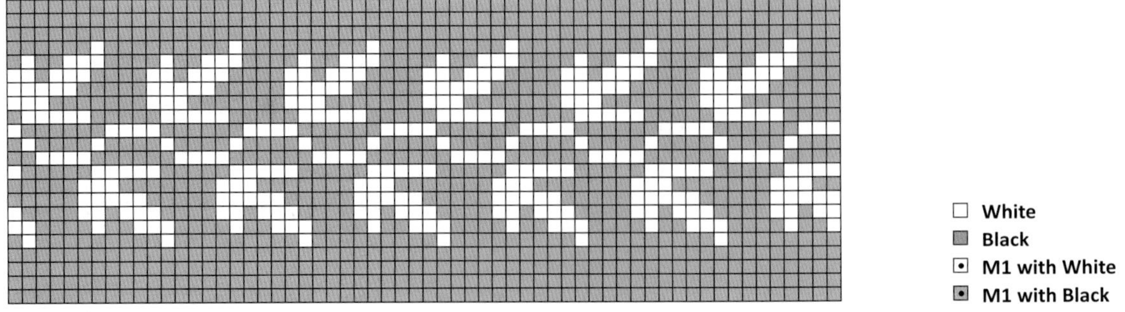
White
Black
M1 with White
M1 with Black

INSTRUCTIONS

Skill Level: Intermediate

SIZES
Women's (Men's)

MATERIALS
Yarn:
CYCA #1 (fingering) Rauma 2-ply Gammelserie
(100% Norwegian wool, 175 yd/160 m / 50 g)

Yarn Colors and Amounts:
Black 436: 100 (100) g
White 401: 50 (50) g

Needles:
U. S. size 0 (1.5) / 2 (2.5) mm: set of 5 dpn

GAUGE
The size is adjusted by changing the gauge/
needle size. Follow the same instructions for
both sizes.
34 (31) sts = 4 in / 10 cm.
Adjust needle size to obtain correct gauge if
necessary.

RIGHT MITTEN
With Black, CO 60 sts. Divide sts evenly onto 4
dpn and join; pm for beginning of rnd. Knit 4
rnds. Work eyelet foldline: (k2tog, yo) around.
Now work cuff pattern following Chart 1.
On the last rnd, increase 1 st in last st = 61
sts. Now work following Chart 2, increasing
for thumb gusset as shown on chart. After
working gusset increases, set aside 19 sts for
thumb (see page 14). Continue, following
chart. Shape top as shown on chart. Cut yarn
and draw end through rem sts; tighten.

THUMB
Pick up and knit 20 + 20 sts = 40 sts total.
Divide sts onto dpn. Work thumb following
Chart 3, making sure that the patterns align.
Cut yarn and draw end through rem sts;
tighten.

LEFT MITTEN
Work as for right mitten, reversing chart so
thumb is on left side of palm.

FINISHING
Fold cuff along eyelet round and sew down
to WS. Weave in all ends neatly on WS.
Gently steam press mittens under
damp pressing cloth.

CHART 3: THUMB

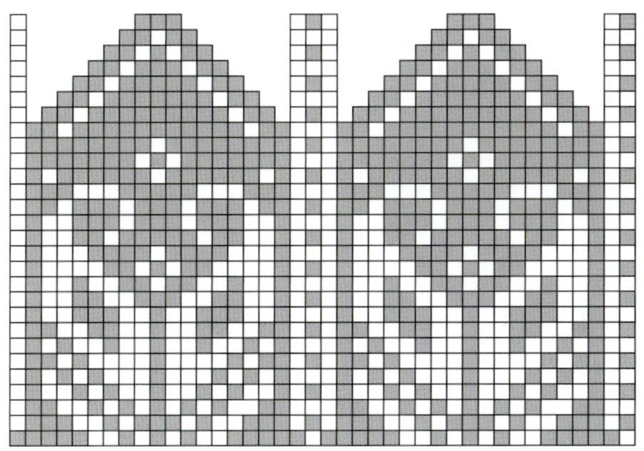

North Wind Mittens

In Selbu, they differentiate between patterns inspired by buck horns and ram horns. Elegant spelsau rams have pretty horns that almost curl into a spiral. "Ram's horn" roses are found on several of the oldest mittens from the village. In order to have room for such fine details, these mittens were knitted with very fine yarn on tiny needles.

I have taken a traditional rose pattern as my starting point, but I changed it slightly; however, I chose to keep the original level of detail, so this design is worked on needles that are U. S. 000 / 1.5 mm. If you don't have a lot of experience with knitting mittens or using very fine needles, this will probably be challenging. I used the same pattern for a cowl, but there it's knitted with a heavier yarn and on larger needles. It's fun to see how the look changes when the materials and needle size change.

CHART 2

Set aside 19 sts for thumb

CHART 1

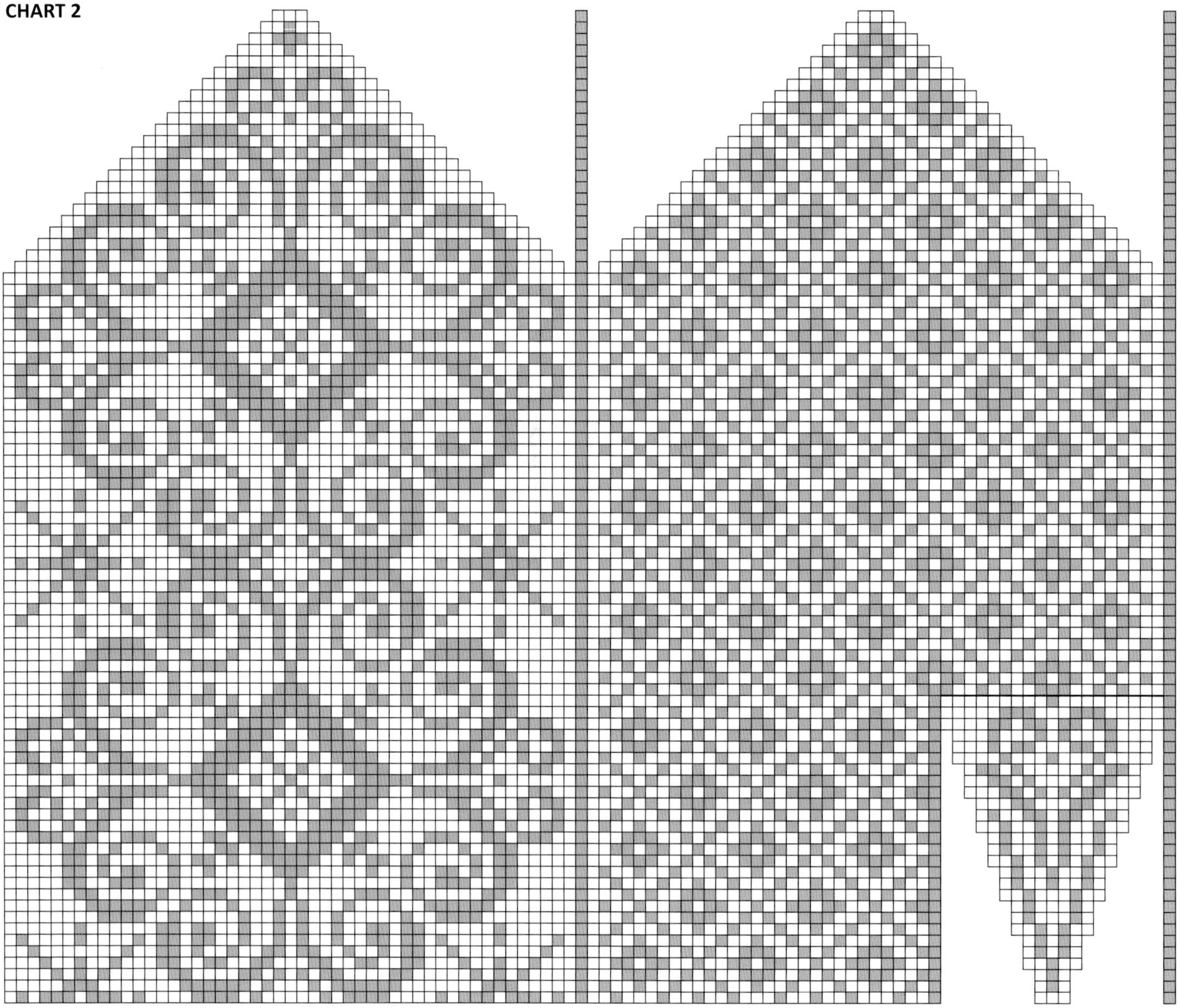

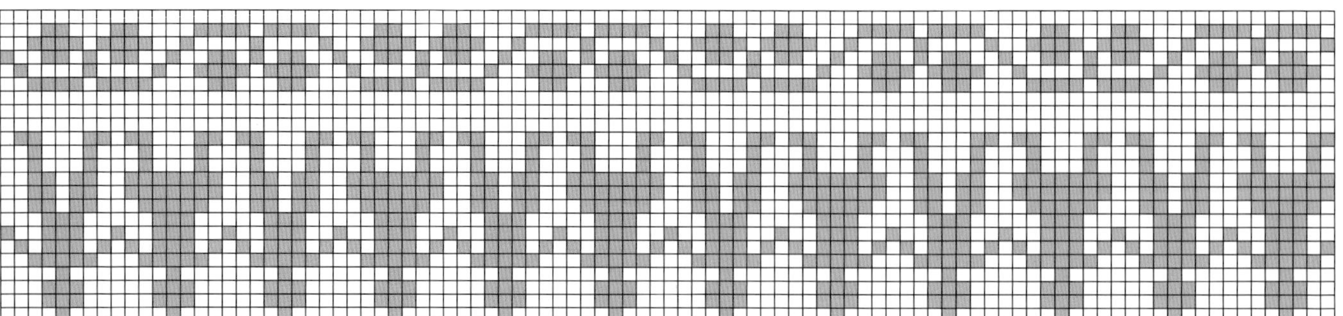

INSTRUCTIONS

Skill Level: Intermediate

SIZES
Women's (Men's)

MATERIALS
Yarn:
CYCA #1 (fingering) Selbu Spinneri Fin Gammel Selbu (100% Norwegian wool, 394 yd/360 m / 100 g)

Yarn Colors and Amounts:
White: 50 (50) g
Medium Gray: 50 (50) g

Needles:
U. S. size 000 (0) / 1.5 (2) mm: set of 5 dpn

GAUGE
The size is adjusted by changing the gauge/needle size. Follow the same instructions for both sizes.
43 (39) sts = 4 in / 10 cm.
Adjust needle size to obtain correct gauge if necessary.

RIGHT MITTEN
With White, CO 96 (96) sts. Divide sts evenly onto 4 dpn and join; pm for beginning of rnd. Knit 5 rnds. Work eyelet foldline: (k2tog, yo) around. Knit 3 rnds and then work cuff pattern following Chart 1. On the last rnd, decrease evenly spaced around to 84 sts. Now work following Chart 2, increasing for thumb gusset as shown on chart. After working gusset increases, set aside 19 sts for thumb (see page 14). Continue, following chart. Shape top as shown on chart. Cut yarn and draw end through rem sts; tighten.

THUMB
Pick up and knit 20 + 20 sts = 40 sts total. Divide sts onto dpn. Work thumb following Chart 3. Cut yarn and draw end through rem sts; tighten.

LEFT MITTEN
Work as for right mitten, reversing chart so thumb is on left side of palm.

FINISHING
Fold cuff along eyelet round and sew down to WS. Weave in all ends neatly on WS. Gently steam press mittens under damp pressing cloth.

□ White
▨ Medium Gray

CHART 3: THUMB

North Wind Cowl

INSTRUCTIONS

FINISHED MEASUREMENTS
Circumference: 37¾ in / 96 cm
Height: 11 in / 28 cm

MATERIALS
Yarn:
CYCA #4 (worsted, afghan, Aran) Hjelholts Uld-spinderi Håndværksgarn (100% Merino wool, 219 yd/200 m / 100 g)

Yarn Colors and Amounts:
Charcoal Gray 04: 100 g
Rowanberry 21: 100 g

Needles:
U. S. size 7 / 4.5 mm: circular: 32 in / 80 cm

GAUGE
20 sts x 22 rnds = 4 x 4 in / 10 x 10 cm.
Adjust needle size to obtain correct gauge if necessary.

COWL
With Rowanberry, CO 192 sts. Join, being careful not to twist cast-on row; pm for beginning of rnd. Work 3 rnds in k2, p2 ribbing and then work in pattern following chart. The repeat is worked 4 times around. After completing charted rows, work 3 rnds k2, p2 ribbing. BO in k2, p2 ribbing.

FINISHING
Weave in all ends neatly on WS. Gently steam press cowl under damp pressing cloth.

□ **Charcoal Gray**
▨ **Rowanberry**

Repeat

North Wind Hat

INSTRUCTIONS

SIZE
One size

MATERIALS
Yarn:
CYCA #4 (worsted, afghan, Aran) Hjelholts Uld-spinderi Håndværksgarn (100% Merino wool, 219 yd/200 m / 100 g)

Yarn Colors and Amounts:
Rowanberry 21: 100 g

Needles:
U. S. size 7 / 4.5 mm: set of 5 dpn

GAUGE
20 sts x 22 rnds = 4 x 4 in / 10 x 10 cm.
Adjust needle size to obtain correct gauge if necessary.

HAT
With Rowanberry, CO 96 sts. Divide sts onto 4 dpn and join, being careful not to twist cast-on row. Work around in k2, p2 ribbing until hat is 8¼ in / 21 cm long.

Shape Crown:
Rnd 1: *K2, p2tog, k2, p2*; rep * to * around.
Rnds 2-5: *K2, p1, k2, p2*; rep * to * around.
Rnd 6: *K2, p1, k2, p2tog*: rep * to * around.
Rnds 7-10: *K2, p1, k2, p1*; rep * to * around.
Rnd 11: *K2tog, p1, k2, p1*: rep * to * around.
Rnds 12-15: *K1, p1, k2, p1*; rep * to * around.
Rnd 16: *K1, p1, k2tog, p1*: rep * to * around.
Rnds 17-20: *K1, p1, k1, p1*; rep * to * around.
Rnd 21: K2tog around.
Cut yarn and draw end through rem sts; tighten.

FINISHING
Weave in all ends neatly on WS. Gently steam press hat under damp pressing cloth.

North Wind Headband

FINISHED MEASUREMENTS
Circumference: 19¾ in / 50 cm

MATERIALS
Yarn:
CYCA #4 (worsted, afghan, Aran) Hjelholts Uld-
spinderi Håndværksgarn (100% Merino wool,
219 yd/200 m / 100 g)

Yarn Colors and Amounts:
Rowanberry 21: 50 g

Needles:
U. S. size 7 / 4.5 mm; cable needle

GAUGE
20 sts x 22 rnds = 4 x 4 in / 10 x 10 cm.
Adjust needle size to obtain correct gauge if
necessary.

HEADBAND
With Rowanberry, CO 25 sts. The band is
worked back and forth.

Set-up Row: K5, p15, k5.
X***Row 1:** Knit.
Row 2: K5, p15, k5*.
Rep * to * 3 times.
Row 7: K10, place next 5 sts on a cable needle
and hold behind work, k5 and then k5 from
cable needle, end k5.
Row 8: Work as for Row 2. Rep * to * 3 times.
Row 15: K5, place next 5 sts on a cable needle
and hold in front of work, k5 and then k5 from
cable needle, end k10.
Row 16: Work as for Row 2. Rep * to * 3
times.X
Rep X-X a total of 8 times.
BO: K2, pass 1st st over 2nd, *k1, pass previous
st over last knitted; rep from * until all sts have
been bound off.

FINISHING
Join short ends of band with mattress st on
RS. Weave in all ends neatly on WS.
Gently steam press headband under
damp pressing cloth.

Cycling Cardigan from Nordland

Charles Ravn (1898-1963) was the only photographer in Ballangen for most of his lifetime. He took photos of local residents of all ages, in both everyday and festive attire. In his photos, we can see that knitted garments were an important part of people's outfits. Cardigans, pullovers, stockings, and mittens were made by women with a thorough knowledge of how to create practical garments that fit well. Many of the garments had lovely details in both shaping and embellishment.

Some of the motifs are recognizable from Annichen Sibbern Bøhn's book *Norwegian Knitting Designs*, first published in Norway in 1929: eight-petal roses, reindeer, dancing men and women, blocks, and wavy shapes. Other garments seem to have their origins in books that came out in the years after.

One sweater in particular fascinated me—a cardigan with a distinctive wave pattern. The photo shows a young boy with a large bicycle. The sweater, without front bands, has been tucked into his trousers. The sleeves are set in. It's difficult to tell from the picture whether the sweater was knit with two or three colors.

I decided to make a variation with raglan shaping. I used two colors throughout, except for a third color on the shoulders to make the sweater a little more distinctive.

INSTRUCTIONS

Skill Level: Experienced

SIZES
S (M, L, XL, XXL)

FINISHED MEASUREMENTS
Chest: 37½ (39½, 42½, 45¾, 48¾) in / 95 (100, 108, 116, 124) cm
Waist: 37½ (39½, 42½, 45¾, 48¾) in / 95 (100, 108, 116, 124) cm
Sleeve Length: 17¾ (17¾, 17¾, 17¾, 17¾) in / 45 (45, 45, 45, 45) cm
Total Length: 26½ (26½, 26½, 28¼, 28¼) in / 67 (67, 67, 72, 72) cm

MATERIALS
Yarn:
CYCA #1 (fingering) Rauma Finull PT2 (100% Norwegian wool, 191 yd/175 m / 50 g)

Yarn Colors and Amounts:
Brown 4111: 250 (250, 300, 300, 350) g
Yellow 4075: 200 (200, 250, 300, 300) g
Pink 466: 50 (50, 50, 50, 50) g

Needles:
U. S. sizes 2.5 and 4 / 3 and 3.5 mm: circulars and sets of 5 dpn

Crochet Hook:
small size

Notions:
9 or 10 buttons

GAUGE
24 sts x 30 rnds = 4 x 4 in / 10 x 10 cm.
Adjust needle size to obtain correct gauge if necessary.

BODY
With Brown and smaller circular, CO 228 (238, 258, 278, 298) sts + 6 extra sts for steek (steek sts are not included in stitch counts; see pages 8 and 12). Join, being careful not to twist cast-on row; pm for beginning of rnd. Work around in k2, p2 ribbing for 1½ in / 4 cm. Change to larger circular and knit 1 rnd, decreasing 1 st = 227 (237, 257, 277, 297) sts rem. Work in pattern following Chart 1 until body measures approx. 17 (17, 17, 18½, 18½) in / 43 (43, 43, 47, 47) cm, ending with a complete repeat. On the last rnd of the repeat,

BO 11 sts at each side for underarms: K55 (58, 63, 68, 73), BO 11 sts, k95 (99, 109, 119, 129), BO 11 sts, k55 (58, 63, 68, 73). Set body aside while you knit sleeves.

SLEEVES
With Brown and smaller dpn, CO 48 (52, 56, 60, 64) sts. Divide sts onto 4 dpn and join; pm for beginning of rnd. Work around in k2, p2 ribbing for 4¼ in / 11 cm. Change to larger dpn and knit 1 rnd, increasing 1 st at center of underarm. Now work in pattern following Chart 2, beginning at arrow for your size. On every 6th rnd, increase 2 sts at center of underarm until sleeve is 17¼ in / 44 cm long and has 87 (91, 95, 99, 103) sts. Make sure you end with a complete repeat to match body. BO 11 sts centered on underarm. Set sleeve aside while you knit second sleeve the same way.

RAGLAN SHAPING
Arrange sleeves and body on long circular = 357 (375, 403, 431, 459) sts total. Pm at each intersection of sleeve and body and continue in pattern *at the same time* as you shape raglan:
*Begin at center front; knit until 2 sts rem on front, k2tog, sl 1 on sleeve, k1, psso; knit until 2 sts rem on sleeve, k2tog, sl 1 on back, k1, psso; knit until 2 sts rem on back, k2tog, sl 1 on sleeve, k1, psso; knit until 2 sts rem on sleeve, k2tog, sl 1 on front, k1, psso and knit rest of front including steek.
Knit next rnd without decreasing.*
Rep * to * 9 (10, 11, 12, 13) times. Continue to decrease the same way but only on the sleeves and not the body. Decrease on every rnd until 18 (20, 22, 24, 26) sts rem on each sleeve. Replace Brown with Pink (see Chart 3). Continuing with Pink to end of body, decrease on sleeves as est until 10 (12, 14, 16, 18) sts rem for each shoulder.

SHOULDER SHAPING
Work each shoulder separately with Pink. Divide work, placing all sts for right side of cardigan on a holder. Place all the sts of left side on one circular. See below for an alternate method of shaping shoulder. *Beginning with sleeve facing you, knit until 1 st rem on sleeve. Knit last st and first st of back tog through back loops, k1; turn. Purl until 1 st rem on sleeve, p2tog, p1; turn.*
X Rep * to * 3 times. On the next

row, knit until 1 st rem on sleeve, knit last st tog tbl with first 2 sts on back, k1; turn. Purl until 1 st rem on sleeve, purl last st tog with next 2 sts of front, p1; turn. X. Rep X to X until you've decreased 23 (25, 27, 30, 32) sts on each side. Place the 10 (12, 14, 16, 18) sts of right shoulder on needle and work to match left shoulder. If you prefer, you can shape the shoulders by working back and forth without decreasing and simply seaming the shoulders. Work back and forth in stockinette on one shoulder for 23 (25, 27, 30, 32) rows. Place sts on a holder while you work opposite shoulder the same way.

FINISHING
Weave in all ends neatly on WS. Crochet a facing or machine-stitch to reinforce steek edges down front. Begin with left front band.
Left Front Band: With Brown and smaller circular, pick up and knit 3 sts for every 4 rows (use crochet hook to make it easier). With smaller circular, work back and forth in k2, p2 ribbing for a total of 8 rows. BO in ribbing.
Right Front Band: Mark spacing of 9 or 10 buttons on left band. With Brown, pick up

and knit sts as for left band (make sure you have the same number of sts). Work back and forth in k2, p2 ribbing. On the 4th row, make buttonholes. Make a buttonhole with BO 2 sts opposite each button marker. On next row, CO 2 sts over each gap. Continue in ribbing you've worked a total of 8 rows. BO in ribbing.

Now carefully cut open steek. Fold facings to WS and sew down neatly to cover cut edges.

Neckband: Pick up and knit sts around neck and shoulder bands. Work 8 rnds k2, p2 ribbing. BO in ribbing.
Edgings: With Pink, crochet along front bands and around neck: Attach yarn with 1 sc, *ch 3, skip 2 sts of ribbing and work 1 sc in third knitted st*. Rep * to * all around, skipping only 1 st in each corner.

Weave in rem ends neatly on WS. Gently steam press cardigan under a damp pressing cloth. Sew on buttons.

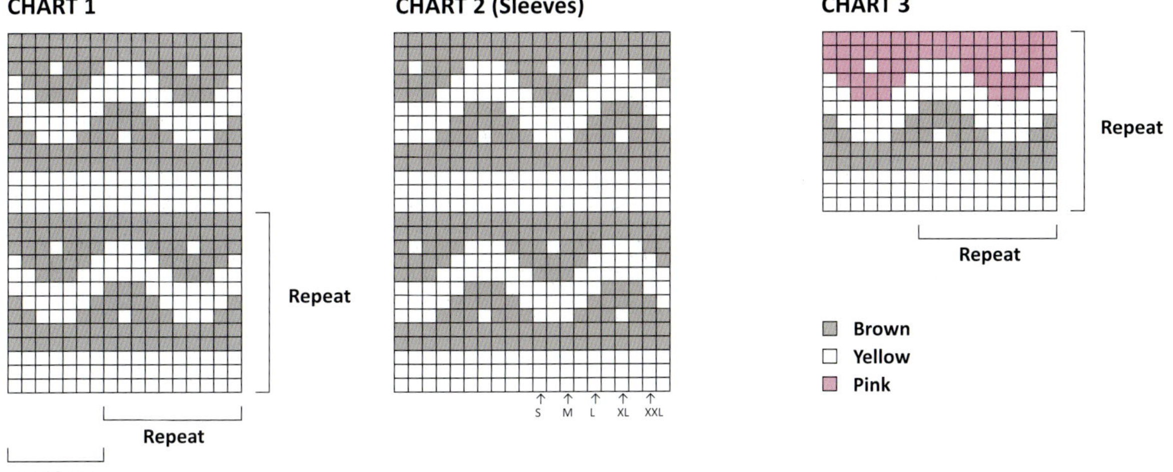

Felted Mittens
with Cabled Cuffs

Fishermen along Norway's long coast used thick felted mittens when they were out to sea. These mittens hold warmth well even when wet. A number of them have been preserved. The shape is quite simple. They might have a few rounds of garter stitch at the lower edge, or perhaps more traditional knit and purl ribbed cuffs. Sometimes there are increases for a thumb gusset; other mittens have straight lower hands. Most often, these mittens have rounded tops, but some do have pointed tips. Initials were often embroidered on with red thread so that men could identify their own pairs of mittens.

By contrast, there are few examples of women's mittens from the northernmost provinces. However, a photo of three women skiing, taken by amateur photographer Signe Wesel Zapffe (1906-1927) at Storskarsfjellet in Troms in 1924, shows that they all wore felted mittens similar to fishermen's mittens. The mittens could also have been Sami.

The Norwegian National Library has 157 photographs taken by Signe, who was the sister of the philosopher and outdoorsman Peter Wessel Zapffe (1899-1990). He also took photos. The siblings grew up in Tromsø; Signe was only 21 years old when she died of tuberculosis.

It's difficult to say precisely how the young women's mittens were made, but I let myself be inspired to make a pair of felted mittens with a cable edging.

CHART 2

CHART 3—THUMB

CHART 1

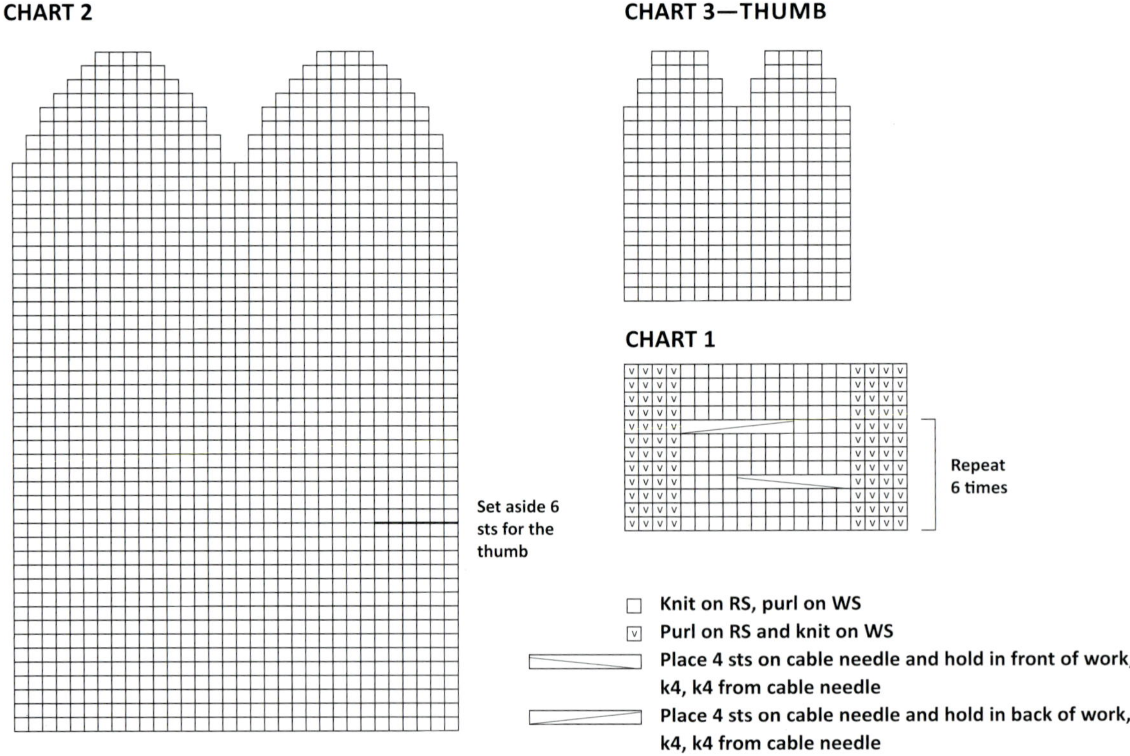

Set aside 6 sts for the thumb

Repeat 6 times

☐ Knit on RS, purl on WS

ⅴ Purl on RS and knit on WS

Place 4 sts on cable needle and hold in front of work, k4, k4 from cable needle

Place 4 sts on cable needle and hold in back of work, k4, k4 from cable needle

INSTRUCTIONS

Skill Level: Beginner/Intermediate

SIZES
Women's

MATERIALS
Yarn:
CYCA #5 (bulky) Rauma Vams PT3 (100% wool, 90 yd/82 m / 50 g)

Yarn Color and Amount:
Sea-Green V52: 150 g

Alternate Yarn:
CYCA #5 (bulky) Sandnes Fritidsgarn (100% wool, 77 yd/70 m / 50 g)

Needles:
U. S. size 10 / 6 mm: set of 5 dpn; cable needle

GAUGE
14 sts in stockinette = 4 in / 10 cm.
Adjust needle size to obtain correct gauge if necessary.

Begin by working the cabled edging back and forth. Next, pick up and knit stitches along one edge and work the mitten in the round as usual.

CABLE EDGING
CO 18 sts and work cable as follows:
WS: K4, p12, k4.
RS: P4, k12, p4.
Continue as shown on Chart 1. Work cable pattern a total of 6 times and end with knit over knit and purl over purl as shown on chart. BO until 1 st rem on needle.

RIGHT MITTEN
Pick up and knit 33 sts along edge of cable strip for a total of 34 sts. Pick up 2 sts for every 3 rows.
Join strip and pm for beginning of rnd. Work (k2tog, yo) around. Knit 4 rnds. Turn work with WS out and work 5 rnds k1, p1. Decrease 1 st at each side = 32 sts rem. Continue, following Chart 2.
At heavy line on chart, set aside 6 sts for thumb. The easiest way to make the thumbhole is to work the 6 sts with smooth con-trast-color scrap yarn, slide the sts back to left needle, and knit them with working yarn (see page 14 for more details).

Continue in stockinette, shaping top as shown on chart. Decrease on right side with sl 1, k1, psso (or ssk). On left side, k2tog. When 8 sts rem, cut yarn and draw end through rem sts; tighten.

THUMB
Pick up and knit 8 + 8 sts around thumbhole = 16 sts total. See page 14 for details. Work thumb following chart. Decrease top as for top of mitten. Cut yarn and draw end through rem sts; tighten.

LEFT MITTEN
Work as for right mitten, reversing chart so thumb is on left side of palm.

FINISHING
Weave in all ends neatly on WS. The finished mittens will be rather large, but will shrink when felted.

FELTING
If you knitted the mittens with Vams or Fritids-garn: Wash the mittens in the washing machine on a short program with water at 104°F / 40°C and regular washing powder (not powder for whitewash). Take them out and shape them while they are still wet. Pull them out a bit at the cable edge. Lay flat to dry.

If you want to have more control over the felting process and size of the mittens, felt them by hand. Fill a pan with warm water, add soap—for example, dishwashing or green soap—and then wash and rub the mittens on a felting board or against each other until they are about the right size. Work with both mittens at the same time. Rub more vigorously lengthwise so they will shrink more in length. It's hard work, and it'll take a while. Continue until mittens are just right. Rinse out soap, shape mittens, and lay flat to dry.

You can also put wet mittens into a spin dryer for felting. Stop the machine at regular intervals so you can see how well they've felted.

Blue and White Half-Gloves

A variety of half-mittens or half-gloves can be worn for work or fine occasions. There are many names for these accessories: wrist warmers, muffettees, mitts, small sleeves, and fingerless gloves or mittens—all covering only the wrists or part of the hands. In work situations, a pair of half-gloves protects against water and other blisters. They are helpful when raking hay or doing other work outdoors. In Norway, these kinds of work gloves are always one color, usually undyed.

Half-gloves were also worn historically for parties and celebrations. They were as prettily embellished as other elegant gloves. Both married and unmarried women wore such accessories for church and kept them on during the service.

Half-gloves have been made using all sorts of techniques and were worn in differing places. They could have been made with white cotton and have lace patterns, or knitted with two colors. They were popular in towns and villages in the second half of the nineteenth century.

Many of them were decorated with beads, all of which had to be threaded onto the yarn in the correct order before knitting began.

Fine yarn ready to have beads threaded on for knitting with quite small needles.

INSTRUCTIONS

Skill Level: Intermediate

SIZES
Women's (Men's)

MATERIALS
Yarn:
CYCA #2 (sport, baby) Hillesvåg ullvarefabrikk Ask (Hifa 2) (100% Norwegian wool, 344 yd/315 m / 100 g)

Yarn Colors and Amounts:
Peasant Blue 316082 or Light Navy Blue 316036: 50 (50) g
Natural White 316057: or Half-Bleached White 316047: 50 (50) g

Alternate Yarn:
CYCA #1 (fingering) Rauma 2-ply Gammelserie (100% Norwegian wool, 175 yd/160 m / 50 g)

Needles:
U. S. size 1.5 (2.5) / 2.5 (3) mm: set of 5 dpn

Notions:
blue and white beads if desired
beading needle and thread

GAUGE
The size is adjusted by changing the gauge/needle size. Follow the same instructions for both sizes.
28 (26) sts = 4 in / 10 cm.
Adjust needle size to obtain correct gauge if necessary.

RIBBING
With Blue, CO 48 sts. Divide sts onto dpn and join. Knit 1 rnd.
Now work 20 rnds: *k1 Blue, p1 Blue, k1 Blue, p1 White*; rep * to * round.

Work 1 rnd: *K1 White, p1 Blue, k2 White*; rep * to * around.

Note: This ribbing is somewhat less elastic than single-color ribbing. If you want a more elastic cuff, work all the ribbing with Blue.

RIGHT HALF-GLOVE
Continue with White. Knit 1 rnd, increasing 3 sts evenly spaced around = 51 sts total. Now work following Chart 1. Increase for thumb gusset as shown on chart to a total of 64 sts. See page 14 for how to set aside the 13 thumb sts. Finish charted rows and then work 5 rnds ribbing as for lower edge. BO with Blue.

Note: There are long yarn floats in the pattern for the back of the hand. You should twist the yarns around each on WS about every 5 sts. It's important that you do not stack the twists above each other.

THUMB
Pick up 15 sts each below and above scrap yarn = 30 sts total. Divide sts onto dpn. Work thumb following Chart 2. Make sure you align the flower over the stem correctly. Finish with 5 rnds ribbing as before. BO with Blue. Cut yarn and draw end through rem sts; tighten.

LEFT HALF-GLOVE
Work as for right half-glove, reversing chart so thumb is on left side of palm.

FINISHING
Weave in all ends neatly on WS. Gently steam press half-gloves under damp pressing cloth. If you want more decorative half-gloves, you can sew on small glass beads.

CHART 1

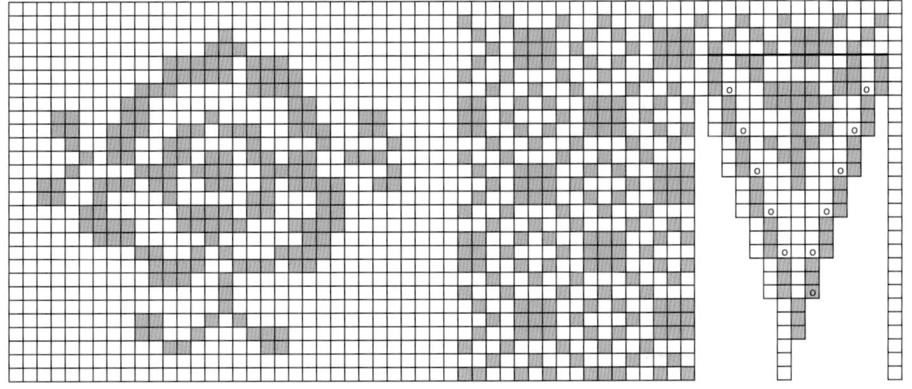

CHART 2: THUMB

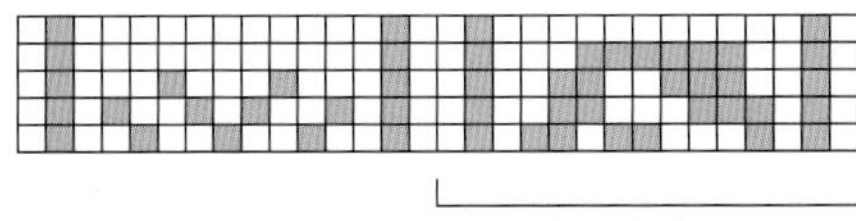

	Blue
	White
	M1 with Blue
	M1 with White

Fishermen's Mittens from Vadsø

Vadsø Museum—Ruija Kvenmuseum (the Museum of Finnish Heritage in Norway) has a pair of felted fishermen's mittens knitted in undyed wool. They're edged with traditional k2, p2 ribbing and have increases for a thumb gusset. The top is nicely rounded.

My version has only one thumb on each hand, but two thumbs each was common on fisherman's mittens. That way they could be worn on either hand or either side so they wore out more evenly. The thumb not in use hung loosely at the side. These days, it would be a surprise to see anyone wearing mittens with two thumbs.

INSTRUCTIONS

Skill Level: Beginner/Intermediate

SIZES
Women's (Men's)

MATERIALS
Yarn:
CYCA #5 (bulky) Rauma Vams PT3 (100% wool, 90 yd/82 m / 50 g)

Yarn Color and Amounts:
Red-Orange V61: 100 (150) g

Needles:
U. S. size 10 (10½) / 6 (7) mm: set of 5 dpn

GAUGE
14 (12) sts in stockinette = 4 in / 10 cm.
Adjust needle size to obtain correct gauge if necessary.

RIGHT MITTEN
CO 36 (40) sts. Divide sts onto 4 dpn and join; pm for beginning of rnd. Work around in k2, p2 ribbing for 3¼ in / 8 cm.

The rest of the mitten is worked in stockinette. Knit 5 rnds. Pm after the first st on first needle. Increase for thumb gusset with M1 on each side of marked st. Knit 5 rnds and then M1 on each side of the 3 thumb sts. Knit 5 rnds and M1 on each side of the 5 thumb sts = 42 (46) sts. Set aside 7 (7) sts for thumb—see page 14 for details.

Continue in stockinette until mitten is 11½ (12¾) in / 29 (32) cm long. Make sure you have the same number of sts for front and back of mitten before you begin top shaping.
K1, sl 1, k1, psso, knit until 3 sts rem on Ndl 2, k2tog: rep * to * on Ndls 3 and 4. Knit 1 rnd. Rep these two rnds 3 times. Now decrease on every rnd until 6 sts rem. Cut yarn and draw end through rem sts; tighten.

THUMB
Pick up and knit 8 + 8 sts around thumbhole = 16 sts total (9 + 9, total of 18 sts). See page 14 for details. Knit around on thumb until it's 2¾ (3¼) in / 7 (8) cm long. Shape as for top of mitten, repeating * to * once; knit 1 rnd and then decrease on every rnd until 6 sts rem. Cut yarn and draw end through rem sts; tighten.

LEFT MITTEN
Work as for right mitten, reversing so thumb is on left side of palm.

FINISHING
Weave in all ends neatly on WS. The finished mittens will be rather large, but will shrink when felted.

FELTING
Wash the mittens in the washing machine on a short program with water at 104°F / 40°C and regular washing powder (not powder for whitewash). Take the mittens out of the machine and shape them while they're still wet. Pull them out a bit at the cable edge. Lay flat to dry.

If you want to have more control over the felting process and size of the mittens, felt them by hand. Fill a pan with warm water, add soap—for example, dishwashing or green soap—and then wash and rub the mittens on a felting board or against each other until they are about the right size. Work with both mittens at the same time. Rub more vigorously lengthwise so they will shrink more in length. It's hard work, and it'll take a while. Continue until mittens are just right. Rinse out soap, shape mittens, and lay flat to dry.

You can also put wet mittens into a spin dryer for felting. Stop the machine at regular intervals so you can see how well they've felted.

YARN INFORMATION

Anzula yarns may be purchased from retailers listed by:
Anzula
anzula.com

Isager Strik yarns may be purchased from retailers listed by:
Knit Isager
knitisager.com

Lofoten yarns are available (with international shipping charges) from:
Lofoten Wool
lofoten-wool.no

Rauma yarns may be purchased from:
The Yarn Guys
theyarnguys.com

The Woolly Thistle
thewoollythistle.com

Sandnes yarns may be purchased (with international shipping charges) from:
Scandinavian Knitting Design
scandinavianknittingdesign.com

Some yarns and materials—Du Store Alpakka, Hillesvag, Hjelholts Uldspinderi, and Sjøling-stad Uldvarefabrik yarns, in particular—may be difficult to find. A variety of additional and substitute yarns are available from:
Webs – America's Yarn Store
75 Service Center Road
Northampton, MA 01060
800-367-9327
yarn.com

LoveKnitting.com
loveknitting.com/us

If you are unable to obtain any of the yarn used in this book, it can be replaced with a yarn of a similar weight and composition. Please note, however, the finished projects may vary slightly from those shown, depending on the yarn used. Try www.yarnsub.com for suggestions.

For more information on selecting or substituting yarn, contact your local yarn shop or an online store; they are familiar with all types of yarns and would be happy to help you. Additionally, the online knitting community at Ravelry.com has forums where you can post questions about specific yarns. Yarns come and go so quickly these days and there are so many beautiful yarns available.

RESOURCES

Bårdsgård, Anne. *Selbu Mittens*. Trafalgar Square Books, 2019.

Sundbø, Annemor. *Koftearven [Sweater Heritage]*. Gyldendal Norsk Forlag, 2019.

Sundbø, Annemor. *Setesdal Sweaters: The History of the Norwegian Lice Pattern*. Torridal Tweed, 2001.

Sæther, Nina Granlund. *Mittens from Around Norway*. Trafalgar Square Books, 2017.

Sæther, Nina Granlund. *Norske strikketradisjoner [Norwegian Knitting Traditions]*. Gyldendal Norsk Forlag, 2019.

Sæther, Nina Granlund. *Socks from Around Norway*. Trafalgar Square Books, 2019.

ABBREVIATIONS

BO — bind off (= UK cast off)
CC — contrast (pattern) color
ch — chain stitch
cm — centimeters
CO — cast on
dpn — double-pointed needles
in — inch(es)
g — grams
k — knit
k2tog — knit 2 together (= 1 stitch decreased; right-leaning decrease)
kb&f — knit into back (as for twisted knit) and then front (as for regular knit) loop of same stitch (= 1 stitch increased)
LLI — left-lifted increase: knit into left side of 2nd st below that on needle
M1R — make 1 right = increase 1 stitch by picking up the strand between 2 stitches with left needle tip, from back to front, and knit into front of strand
M1 — make 1 or M1L = increase 1 stitch by picking up the strand between two stitches with the left needle tip, from front to back, and knit directly into back loop. This makes a left-leaning increase.
M1p — make 1 purlwise = increase 1 stitch by picking up the strand between two stitches with the left needle tip, from back to front, and purl directly into front loop (= right-leaning increase); for left-leaning increase, pick up strand from front to back and purl into back loop
m — meters
MC — main (background) color
mm — millimeters
p — purl
pm — place marker

psso — pass slipped stitch over
puk — pick up and knit
rem — remain(s)(ing)
rep — repeat
RLI — right-lifted increase: knit into right side of st below st on needle and then knit st on needle
RS — right side
sc — single crochet (= British double crochet)
sl — slip
sl m — slip marker
sl st — slip stitch
ssk — [slip 1 knitwise] 2 times, knit the 2 sts together through back loops (= 1 stitch decreased; left-leaning decrease)
st(s) — stitch(es)
tbl — through back loop(s)
tog — together
WS — wrong side
Wyb — with yarn held in back
wyf — with yarn held in front
yd — yard(s)
yo — yarnover
– — repeat the sequence between the asterisks
steek — a section of extra stitches added so that you can knit in the round on a sweater body that will later be cut open for the two fronts of a cardigan or for the armholes from underarms to shoulders, or for the neck (for example, a placket). Instructions for working the steek stitches and for reinforcing and cutting a steek are given in individual patterns. Usually the steek stitches are worked in alternating pattern colors or with one color for single-color row.

PHOTOGRAPHY CREDITS

All photos by Elvind Røhne except the following:

Guri Pfeifer, pages 11, 15, 20.

Nina Granlund Sæther, pages 9, 11, 12, 13, 14, 72, 74, 91, 112, 124, 130, 132, 138, 142, 146.

page 16, Øyvind Andersen / Folkenberg Museum

page 26, Getty Research Institute

page 32, Anne-Lise Reinsfelt / Norwegian Folk Museum

page 36, Mittet & Co AS / National Library

page 40, Anne-Lise Reinsfelt / Norwegian Folk Museum

page 46, Gustav Borgen / Norwegian Folk Museum

page 50, Norwegian Folk Museum

page 54, Norwegian Institute for Bunad and Folk Costumes

page 58, Nils J. Engebretsen / Norwegian Folk Museum

page 64, Lågdal Museum

page 68, Larvik Museum

page 76, Anno Domkirkeodden [Cathedral Point]

page 80, Anne-Lise Reinfelt / Norwegian Folk Museum

page 84, Ingebjørg Vegestog's Collection / Heimar og folk in Bykle

page 86, Gunnar Å. Helle / Setesdal Museum

page 94, Knud Knudsen / University Library in Bergen

page 98, Haugaland Museum

page 102, Haugaland Museum

page 106, Lauritz Johan Berkker Larsen / University Library in Bergen

page 110, Marcus Seilmer / University Library in Bergen

page 114, University Museum in Bergen

page 118, Knud Knudsen / University Library in Bergen

page 122, Marcus Seilmer / Norwegian Folk Museum

page 126, Marcus Seilmer / Norwegian Folk Museum

page 134, The Nordmøre Museum Foundation

page 156, Charles Ravn / Archive of Charles Ravn / Archive in Nordland

page 160, Signe Wessel Zappfe / National Library

page 164, Anne-Lise Reinsfelt / Norwegian Folk Museum

page 168, Vadsø Museum—Ruija (Museum of Finnish Heritage in Norway)